MA

To Mike

Enjoy!

Fondly,
Rosemary

Spilling My Guts

**A Poetic Journey
of Healing**

Spilling My Guts

A Poetic Journey of Healing

Rosemary S. McGee

ARSEYA PUBLISHING • NEW JERSEY

Library of Congress Control Number: 2001012345

ISBN-13   978-0-9745185-5-8
ISBN-10   0-9745185-5-7

Cover and book design by Curtis Tow Graphics, New York, NY

Printed in the United States by The Wall Street Group, Inc.

Published in the United States by Arseya Publishing
New Vernon, New Jersey
www.arseya.com

FIRST EDITION

For Dennis
For Darin
For Phil
For Mom and Dad

Contents

Preface

I had what I thought to be a reasonably normal childhood, growing up in a moderate middle class family, attending public school, playing with friends, sitting on the curb reading comic books, sneaking out at night when I was a teen. When I was out of line, I was punished. I never really thought about whether my parents were better or worse than my friends' parents, I guess I thought most kids were treated the same as I was. I didn't know then the affect deep family secrets and minor abuses, both verbal and physical would have on me, my self esteem and my ability to love myself.

Over the past two years, I have come face-to-face with many aspects of my life from my childhood, my teens, my first marriage, and the death of loved ones. Each situation had to be addressed. My way of working through them was by reliving them, by writing my way through them in poetry. My poems are interspersed within the relevant parts of my story, attempting to reveal how I thought of each situation as I looked back and tried to make sense of it. As I wrote, I recreated the time or the scene, often feeling as I did when I was in the middle of it. Living it again as an adult, being open to my shortcomings and the foibles of others, allowed me to forgive and let go. Reliving and writing each event also gave me control of the memory. As I wrote, I was reordering my memories and removing the emotional charge, the hair trigger that could set me off years, decades later.

Once in a while when I'm reading a good book a passage will catch me and cut to the quick. It is the truth of what I read that has such power. Frederick Buechner, in his book *Telling Secrets* caught me one day as I sat reading in my airplane seat. One minute calm and sane, the next sobbing, awash with tears. He was saying that we are all born with an original, true self which gets lost as the world has its way with us. I really liked the sound of that. He went on to say that this true self, no matter how deeply it gets buried, is still who we really are at our core, and is always available to us. Many view this as our unconscious mind, or soul or spirit, which contains the wisdom of the ages, the answers we often search for, the knowledge to heal us, if only we would look for it. As I read, the truth that I was not living out of my true self sprang from the pages and filled me with sorrow, fear, and remorse and a resoluteness to figure it out, to find that luminous self of mine and become the woman I was put on earth to be.

Telling our secrets, our stories, is a means of getting to some of our most deeply hidden thoughts, feelings, and memories. Writing about them is a way of working out past events or inner conflicts on a multi-dimensional level and often serves as a catharsis or cleansing as we gain insight into our selves. Your stories and your secrets are different from mine. Perhaps not as bad. Perhaps you have had lower lows and have deeper scars. What matters is having the desire, the willingness to put it all behind us. The healing starts when we pick up our pen.

Writing is a way to claim our own voice. It can be an effective method of treatment for many ailments, both emotional and physical. Chemical and hormonal changes take place within our brain and our body when we write and have lasting positive affects. Current problems and past traumas that seem to have power over us are diffused and discharged through the act of writing. When we write, open our hearts and let them bleed on the page, we are freed of the demons that haunt us. They bubble up from the alembic, from deep in our unconscious minds, from our memories and our dreams, and as the ink dries on the paper, they become light, lose their hold on us and slowly drift away.

Simply put, this book is about how I used writing, specifically poetry, as a means of healing with the goal of letting go and moving on. It is about digging down, exhuming that buried self, understanding and accepting the past. It is about forgiving myself and others, taking my spirit back, and getting on with my life. Perhaps you will find something between the covers of this book that resonates within you and moves you to write. Pain is what finally motivated me. Either way, I hope you enjoy my story.

A few names have been changed to maintain the privacy of others.

CHAPTER ONE

The Original Sin

M arian was sickly. Don't misunderstand though, she may have been physically weak, but she was always mentally strong. She had the mind of a detective, saw everything and recorded it for later use. When you hide things, you become adept at seeing what's hidden. Marian, my mother, always worked hard. She held men's jobs in an era when that was unfashionable. What Mom really was, was unhappy, sometimes to the point of being hateful especially toward my father, Scob. She also believed herself to be a martyr of sorts.

I have a strong belief that pain, disease and illness begin as small seeds of inner unrest that germinate and flourish in the compost of guilt, shame and fear. I often wondered what was at the core of Mom's physical maladies and her fiery resentfulness toward Dad, but I could never figure it out. Not until Dad died that is, and Mom came to live with me and Phil, my husband of eighteen months.

Mom and Dad were inveterate liars. It was a habit they practiced and perfected which I observed throughout my life with them. They would lie for no reason, just to keep everyone guessing, and keep them from getting too close. Mom had always handled the family financials, paid the bills, kept thorough and accurate files of documents and notations surely to be needed sometime in the future. We left Phoenix with Mom, a few boxes of her most important files, and Dad's ashes in a duffel bag. Once she got settled into her new home and routine, we had to deal with the formalities of death. I made an appointment with the Social Security office so we could officially report Dad's passing, and was going to begin calling and writing the holders of insurance policies and Honeywell regarding Dad's pension. I cannot say whether it was because Mom was overcome with the pain and grief of Dad's death, or the fear of being found out as I rifled through her legal documents, or both, but about a week after her arrival Mom revealed her secret.

Seventy-eight, frail, weakened by recent surgery, uprooted from her home to mine, grieving the death of the only man she ever loved and hated, sobbing, her head in her hands, my mother confessed her sin. When I recall that moment when the words bubbled up her throat and out of her mouth, I see her image sitting in the chair in our living room. I had no idea what she was struggling to say, but I gave her my attention, telling her that whatever it was, it was ok. Her hands were wringing in her lap, her thin face almost skeletal, her skin transparent, revealing veins through her gentle wrinkles, her lips quivering. Then she said it. She and Dad gave away a baby boy before they were married.

I was shocked, reeling, my head spinning. My sister and I have a brother. Not a half-brother, but a full brother. I never suspected anything like that. She didn't say too much, other than she had prayed for him every day for 55 years, and after the deed was done, she and Dad had never talked about it. I asked did she want to search for him. "Oh my God, no!" was her reply. She was bound by law never to do so. Mom wouldn't answer any more of my questions, and I had many. She got the words out, and that was it. The poor little thing was exhausted and went to bed. She swore me to secrecy. I could not tell my sister or anyone else. This sin, this secret, once uttered, was spoken of only once more on his next birthday.

That crucial act, the birthing and abandoning of their child, their only son, laid the foundation for their lifetime of lying and deceit. It created a family environment with an ever-present undercurrent of tension for us who were not abandoned and I believe, was the root cause of Mom's life-long string of illnesses. The light bulb experiences, the "ahas" that began for me as her confession fell from her lips have continued for me and my sister. The effects of our childhood conditioning and imprinting by our parents, whose behavior was rooted in deceit, guilt, hatred, and resentment, are so deeply ingrained, I imagine we will feel the reverberations for the rest of our lives. The gift Mom gave us is that now we can name it, him, and try to understand. I sat, eyes closed, put on Mom's shoes, and wrote *Son, My Son*. It is dedicated to the Mothers of Borgess, the hospital where Mom lived and worked while pregnant; where she gave birth to and gave away her son.

SON, MY SON

Son, My Son
My God,
What have I done?
How could I suffer the embarrassment?
How could I look them in the eye
And know
They know
And stand tall?

The church,
To keep you was a sin
What would they all say?
What would they all think?
How could I face them?
How could I hold my head high?
How could I love you
And hate you
For my scorn?

Son, My Son
My God,
What have I done?
How could I have known
The emptiness in my soul?
How could I have known
The sadness
The guilt
The shame
I would feel?
How could I have known
The fear I would feel
For you
My Son,
My only Son?

I had to do it
There was no other way
I was alone
I was a woman
I would be scorned
My friends
My family
The church
To keep you was a sin.

You were a baby
You were alone
I was weak
I was selfish
I was afraid
I could not stand up
For what my heart screamed.

I abandoned you
I took the easy way
How could I have known
You would haunt me
All my life?
How could this be right
In the eyes
Of the church?
How could this be right
In the eyes
Of God?

Son, My Son
My God,
What have I done?

Mom died the following May, after three consecutive bouts with pneumonia. My sister Diane had arrived a few days before, and her family had come from California for the funeral. The night of Mom's funeral, our reminiscing turned to inconsistencies and some confusion. I knew it was time for me to tell Diane Mom's secret. I took her into my bedroom so we could talk. She sat on my bed in disbelief. I had had two years for this reality to sink in. Diane, hearing this in the throes of Mom's death was left somewhat in shock. Our heads spun with the realization of having a brother and all the implications it had held throughout our childhoods. Even though I could understand the situation intellectually on an impersonal level, when I tried to put this incredible event in the context of our years as children, teens, and as adults, I found it difficult to reconcile. *Mother or Monster* is extremely judgmental, but expresses what I thought about Mom at that time.

MOTHER OR MONSTER

How does a woman
Having given away
Her firstborn son
Threaten her daughters
"Be good or we'll
Give you away!"

How does a woman
Blame her sorry state of affairs,
Her misery, her unhappiness
Her resentful, loveless marriage
On her children?
"If it weren't for you
I would have left
Long ago."

How does a woman
After suffering most of her life
With guilt
Unwed mother
Child abandoned
Buckling under the weight
Her partner in crime dead,
Tell her secret,
Confess, repent
Free her soul,
Yet, insist on silence, again
Keep the secret hidden?

Upon her death,
Her secret revealed,
Light, sun seeps
Into dank, dark family corners,
Slowly illuminating,
Enlightening.
With understanding,
Old, open wounds knit and heal
Air is once again breathed deeply
False self perceptions are shed
Life begins again.

Diane and I decided we would not try to find this brother of ours. He's a complete stranger, and we could only imagine that he would expect something from us or think we owed him something. The thought of a long lost relative showing up who we then could not get rid of was distasteful and even frightening. We decided we would tell our families, especially our children about him. I knew I could not harbor Mom's secret for her. It had to be told so its power over us would dissipate. We didn't want to paint Mom as a slut or she and Dad as bad people in anyway. We just wanted to tell the truth and we wanted to make her human to them and to us. This brother floated through my mind and in contemplating the magnitude of it all I wrote *Brother.*

BROTHER

Who are you?
Where are you?
How have you lived
All these years?
Were your parents
Kind to you?
Did they love you?
You them?

Fifty-five years
Your mother prayed for you
Fifty-five years
Your mother cried for you
The loss of you
Was all of our losses
The secret of you
Began a life of deceit
Resentment
Illness.
You have had much power
In the lives of these strangers
Your family.

How will we know you?
Will you look like Dad?
Will you look like me?
Do you even know
That we exist?
Is this secret so dark
That it is hidden
Even from you?
Brother
Stranger
Blood
What does it mean?

Who are you?
Where are you?
Do you want to be found?
Come forward
Into the light
Break the spell
End the mystery
Tell the secret.

The thought of Mom secretly and silently praying for her son every day since his birth stuck in my mind and weighed heavily on me. After writing these poems, I found myself thinking of him. I remember including him in my nightly prayers and realized that I was haunted by him. I was not going to take over where Mom left off, praying for a ghost. It was then that I knew I must try to find him. Oddly enough, I have a friend Joe, who is an adoption private eye. My parents were both born and raised in Michigan. I was born there, too, but we moved to Phoenix when I was 7. I had snippets of stories from their childhoods and early adulthood, but no idea where to begin. In one of Mom's old files, I found a mention of his birth year, a crucial piece of information. After writing many letters to counties in Michigan, Joe soon identified the agency that handled my mother's case. Michigan has laws regarding adoption privacy, and I then needed to petition the courts to continue the search. About a year after Mom's death, my brother was located by a court appointed intermediary, Julie. She called and actually spoke with my brother. He was married, had children and grandchildren. He told Julie he had a fine life and wanted no part of me or mine. She said he seemed angry that his parents had given him away and later married each other. He was angry that Mom and Dad had never tried to find him even though they had legally sworn they never would. I was a little sad and rejected that he didn't want to at least talk to me, but eventually I was satisfied that I had found him and knew that Mom could now rest in peace. If he ever changes his mind, my whereabouts are in his file. Julie told me he had a hearty

but rather goofy laugh. That is all I have ever heard about him, and
I do not know his name or whereabouts. The name on his first birth
certificate was *James Thomas*.

JAMES THOMAS

I know that's not your name
It is the name Mom and Dad gave you
Before they gave you
Away.

At first
I didn't want to find you
You're a stranger.
In time
Mom's 55 years praying for you
Wheedled into my mind.

For her, for you
Perhaps for me
I began searching.
Your birth date
All I had to go on.
My friend Joe, Adoption PI
Worked his magic.
Catholic Social Services had Mom's file
Knew the truth.

Your name, whereabouts
Protected by law
Petition courts
Hire intermediary
Locate you
Contact you.

So close
She actually talked to you
Heard your voice
Heard you laugh.
You're married
Have kids, grandkids
My nieces, nephews, grands.
You are ok.
Have a job, a life.

You checked your files eight years before
Angry, hurt
Birth parents married
Didn't keep you
Never looked for you
You looked no further.

Don't you know
They signed away their rights to you
Swore silent oaths
Buried their past.

What turned you away from me, us
Your two sisters?
Anger
Sadness
Indifference?
You said,
You have no interest in knowing us
Only living souls left to tell the story
Your parents
Our life
Life you missed out on.

Perhaps you don't care
Perhaps your life was better anyway
Perhaps there's no going back
For you.

Blood is thicker
And darker than water.
Perhaps too dark.

Knowing

A couple of years ago, I was on a sailing trip in the British Virgin Islands with my husband Phil, and two other couples. Phil and I don't really like sailing. We love the water, the air, and the beaches, but living on the open seas confined on a sailboat for a week just has never interested us. My distaste goes back to a salmon fishing trip I took in 1984 off the coast of San Francisco. The small vessel sailed out through the Golden Gate with 15 foot swells rising, almost capsizing the boat. I started chumming over the side of the boat an hour into the 6 hour sail. I had always loved rollercoaster rides, and I didn't understand why I was getting so sick. The old salts who were on the ship with me were kind and said even they were feeling queasy. I spent most of the next few hours in the tiny ship bathroom with diarrhea and vomiting. I was either kneeling with my face in the pump-flush commode or sitting, banging my head on the wall in front of me as the boat rocked violently.

Phil and I decided to go after all, for the camaraderie and the adventure. Phil had given me a new journal for the trip, and once we set sail, I sat down to write, thinking I would keep a journal of our days at sea. My entry was dull and I was about to put the book down, when a string of different thoughts came to mind. Struck by the Muse, I wrote the first of fourteen poems written during our voyage. I had fun doing it and believe me the colorful, crazy crowd we were with gave me plenty of material.

Most of my writing during that time was light and funny, but on the third day my writing took a turn. Phil's feet were swollen from inactivity, another reason he hates sailing, and he was anxious to do something about it. As we docked at the Bitter End Yacht Club on the island of Jost Van Dyke, he and I immediately took off for a run. Half way into the run, my knee was killing me. It had been bothering me for over a year, sometimes much worse than others. This day it was particularly bad and I began limping along feeling distressed and depressed.

In the core of my being, I knew there was nothing physically wrong with my knee. I had not had an accident nor twisted it in any way. I have been working out for over 25 years, jogging, practicing yoga, skiing, and a variety of other activities. I also fully subscribed to a concept of pain that indicated my mind was distracting me from psychic pain by diverting my attention to physical pain. When we got back on the boat, I picked up my journal and wrote *Knee*.

KNEE

I am strong warrior woman
I can do anything
My knee hurts.
Walk, run, stand
My knee hurts.

I have done so much
Fearlessly
Took risks
Many would not.
Raise children
Build empires
Hike the Canyon
Ski the Alps
Rock climb Yosemite.
Only now
After it all
My knee hurts.

Is this my truth?
My past
Who I was
Who I have been?
I do love her.
Perhaps
I am not her
Anymore.

As *The Mission* plays
I feel the pain of death
I climb the rainforest canopy
I repent.
I feed the poor
I pray for peace
I die for my beliefs.

My truth is
Who I am right now.
My truth is
Who I will be
When I get where I'm going.

I must fear not.
I am not alone
Anymore.
Risks,
Take them.
Commit.

Step forward.
Step forward.
My knee
Will support me
My knee will carry me
Painlessly.

Step forward
Into light
Into a new day
Into my truth.

When I write, the truth spills from my pen. I can lie to myself and others when I speak, but when I write, something mysterious happens. I don't necessarily even think about what I'm writing. Words leak in ink onto the page. Phil was sitting and reading as we were sailing along, and I sat next to him wanting to share this poem with him. I completely choked up as I was reading about letting go of my old perception of myself, of not being alone anymore. That had not happened when I wrote, but when I spoke the words aloud to Phil I was caught by their truth. I was revealed in my stark nakedness. We had been married for nearly seven years, but the old idea of who I was: a single mother raising two boys, building a career, maintaining a household — alone, was still stuck in my mind. Reading those words was an awakening. A mirror appeared in front of me and I was able to see what I could not see before. It had not entirely sunken in, but at that moment I knew I could ask for help and heal my knee. One of the women we were sailing with had seen me reading to Phil. She shared with me later that as she looked up at us, she got the feeling that I was upset and at the same moment, saw what she called the Holy Spirit hovering over my head. It was at the moment that I choked up speaking of letting go of my aloneness that she had the vision. A couple of months went by before the whole experience gelled for me in this poem, *Spirit Within*.

SPIRIT WITHIN

Miracles occur daily
All around us
When we least expect
When we are not looking
Miracles are spiritual awakenings
When we are willing to see.

A miracle occurred on our Ship of Fools
Divine Spirit flashed
Glimpsed by another, as I
Spoke long hidden disguised truth
My realization, awakening
Naked eye obvious.

Wondering
Pondering
How often my miracles
I have missed
Unwilling, unready
Closed to possibilities?
How often my mind's eye
Blinded by arrogance
Closed tight by fear
Afire with anger
Clouded by judgment, resentment?

I choose this time
Listen with a wide open heart
Hear words I speak
Believe in myself
Seek guidance
Dig deeper.

I choose this time
Surrender arms
Weapons of self destruction
Seven Deadly Sins.
Wield instead
Instruments of peace
Humility replacing ego
Patience for haste
Gratefulness and love knocking
Hateful chip off my shoulder.

My heart in my throat,
I choke
Close down
Go silent
Extinguish my voice.
My throat in my heart,
I weep of brokenness
I sing of laughter and joy.

Fuel my spirit
Let it burn brightly
Warm me
Light my path, that
I become a beacon for others
Lost in their darkness.

I believe that illness, disease and pain are things I bring on myself. They are caused by my stress, fear, shame, and guilt, fueled by my secrets and lies, and are hidden behind my masked, inauthentic façade. I learned this over time, but the awakening began as a dawning of my identity as a strong and capable woman coming into her own. The lesson I had to learn split our family like a San Francisco earthquake, with aftershocks lasting for years.

I was twenty-four, and had been having intermittent diarrhea and constipation accompanied with severe cramping for about six months. It had started shortly after our first son Dennis was born, as my husband Ron and I were driving to Phoenix to spend Thanksgiving with our families. It was about a sixteen hour trip from San Francisco and we had planned to drive all night, trading off every three hours or so. Aside from showing off our one month old son to the family, the other reason we were going was to trade our car, a 1970 Mustang for a used Cadillac Eldorado. I hated this idea. It made me feel like a phony, since we had no money and now we were going to drive around in a big flashy pimp-mobile. My dad, another Cadillac driver had found this great car that Ron just had to have.

We began the journey at around four pm on Wednesday afternoon. Dennis was in the backseat in a baby bathtub. There were no laws regulating infant travel in 1975. We were headed southeast on I95, through Bakersfield. We stopped at a rest area, and Ron decided to have a burrito from a food wagon parked there. It wasn't long before he began to have stomach cramps and I needed to take over the wheel. Needless to say, he was useless for the rest of the trip, weak and sick. We made very few stops. Ron would periodically hold Dennis across my lap so I could breast feed him. It was a grueling drive. I was exhausted.

As the sun began to rise in the arid Arizona desert sky I was pulled off the highway, squatting on the side of the road, dealing with the first of many bouts of diarrhea I had that weekend. When we arrived in Phoenix, my mother-in-law who had been against our marriage, grabbed up the heir to the family name and scolded that I couldn't possibly have enough milk to satisfy this hungry baby. The trip was emotional, filled with bouts of joy counterbalanced with demoralization, which culminated on our trip back home in the Caddy. That car. The beginning of the end.

By April of the following year, plagued with what would eventually be diagnosed as Irritable Bowel Syndrome, I decided to seek help. After submitting to an upper and lower GI-Series and a colonoscopy, and feeling as if I had been sexually violated, no physiological cause was found, like worms or Giardia, hence the "We have no idea," IBS diagnosis. I knew the cause. My marriage sucked. Perhaps it was wrong from the start, it was definitely wrong now. I could not, would not say that to the kind physician when he asked me if I was under any undue stress, but I knew the truth in my guts, and they were talking even thought I wasn't.

My mother, had had colon surgery when I was twelve, she was 45. Her malady was called Ileitis, which is now referred to as Crohn's Disease. One-third of her intestine was removed, and for years after she was miserable most of the time. Leaving Presbyterian Hospital in San Francisco after having those tests, I vowed I would not end up like my mother no matter what, and decided to change my attitude. I took Ron off the pedestal I had put him on, and looked at him rationally. In doing so, I stopped negating myself, chucking my feelings, and always assuming that he was right and I was wrong. I began to trust my instincts, what I knew to be true, and stopped subordinating myself, selling myself short and selling myself out.

I know now, that what I did was begin to take back my spirit from this man I had married. My spirit that I had willingly given to him because I thought he was better than I was, all knowing, wise, and wonderful. I felt I was lucky that he put up with me at all, let alone love me. He was 15 years my senior. He had married a nineteen-year old little girl who was beginning to grow up. As my symptoms subsided, I confirmed what I knew at the deepest level of my knowing. Call it psychic, call it intuition, but I knew, at what seemed to be a cellular level, that I controlled whether or not I would suffer from colitis, Irritable Bowel Syndrome, Crone's or anything else. I swore, "Never again!" It took three more years for me to really understand and act on my feelings. My maturing and emotional growth began to soar. I began to understand who I was, or at least get glimpses, the beginnings of self-knowledge and self love. As I remembered that time of coming into my own, I wrote *Incarnation*.

INCARNATION

Born,
Dragon goddess under Taurus sun
Soul truths stamped
God's thumbprint on my psyche
Goodness greatness destined.
Bold, bright determined survivor
Strength, wit, wonder-filled.

Parents chosen,
Beautiful child tide-tossed
Unconscious imprinted
Emotions conditioned
Life lessons learned slowly
Living out legacies.

Ancestral seeds sown
Fear of the future
Shame of the past
Self doubt
Fertilized,
Cross-pollinated
Generation after
Generation.

Original gifts
Hidden under mired layers
Swallowed in quicksand
Shattered by land mines.
Careful stepping
Impedes progress

Jump both feet
Head long, head strong.
Gut-feeling danger signs ignored
Vision blurred by righteousness and rage.

Impulsive decisions, bad choices
Weave tattered tapestry
Ancestral seeds
Sprout crooked beanstalk
Deep roots hold fast
Life lessons learned slowly.

Occasional glimpse
Beautiful child's innocence
Young woman's wonder
Blue moon insights
Stir dragon-bull spirit
Incarnated destiny long dormant
Emerges, daffodils poking
Up through frozen ground
Surrounded by melting snow.

Birth-moment thumbprint riches
Native wisdom, innate character
Surface, swirl, entwine with
Teeming life experience
Worlds weave, merge, meld
Nurture-nature forces unite
Mingled rebirth.

CHAPTER THREE

I Don't Have Rage

R eturning home after our sailing trip, I kept running, even though sometimes I limped along the entire road. As I ran, I would repeat things like, "There is nothing wrong with my knee," or "I have perfect knees," or "I am getting stronger and stronger," but the pain did not stop. Dr. John E. Sarno has a theory about pain, back pain, knee pain, rotator cuff, and more. He is a world renowned specialist who works out of the New York University Rusk Institute for Rehabilitation Medicine. He has written many books on the subject and I had read and reread his, *The Mindbody Prescription*, which explained his theory about how the unconscious mind works, repressing rage and anger associated with incidents and situations from birth forward throughout our lives. When these repressed feelings try to come to consciousness, our unconscious mind, fearing it is too much for us, diverts us by causing us physical pain. Part of the healing is fully believing that there is nothing physically wrong, and living and moving through the pain. I embarked on this determined path to heal my knee through understanding and healing my spirit.

MY MIND, MY BODY

Connection
Mind – Body exists
From man's beginning.
Great minds
I think therefore I am.
We are
What we think we are
Herein lies the problem.

Conscious mind outwardly healthy
No need to look further
Dredge up the past
Boxed and attic stored.
Our mind has a mind
Of its own
Subconscious
Everyday discomfort hiding place
Unconscious
Rage cold storage,
The Great Protector.

Alas! Freud, Jung
Whatever can we do?
If we are willing,
If we are courageous enough
Lift Pandora's box lid
Peer inside
Understand
Accept the dark side
Conscious mind once again
Controls blessed trinity.
Heal the spirit
Mind body follows.

C oming to the realization that I was no longer alone, and could ask for help, I made the decision to seek out a therapist or counselor. I had gone to a psychotherapist once before, when I was 27 and in the middle of my divorce from Ron. At that time, I felt like I was nearing a breakdown, crying in the car as I drove back and forth to work, overwhelmed with guilt and fear. I had gone to see Margaret, a woman I met at a very California non-threatening couples group five years before. Margaret had a unique Jungian/Gestalt treatment regimen she called an Intensive, which took place while living in a studio on her property at Muir Beach. The treatment period lasted between 5 and 10 days depending on how sick you were. I would have therapy sessions with her 2 to 3 times daily and do whatever homework she prescribed: reading, writing, art therapy, or just walking on the beach. Her rules — No newspapers, no TV, no booze, no drugs. So there I was just me, my thoughts, the ocean, and Margaret. I left there after the best part of a week feeling new, relieved, and able to face whatever came my way, including my parents. During the week, one thing I did was listened to what Margaret called the *liar's tapes*, a dialog of family stories and situations that tend to lead the children to doubt themselves, their intuition, their gut feelings of what is true, of what is.

My parents were coming for a visit. In fact, I was driving from Muir Beach to the airport to pick them up. Having just purged myself of all the crap they had implanted within me, needless to say, I was a little apprehensive. It was weird to see them in the flesh, but good too, because I loved them. We all went out for lunch, my parents, my two boys and I. Sitting in a booth at our favorite Mexican restaurant, my father took the paper off his straw, wadded it up and dropped it on the floor. Dennis, observant and inquisitive child that he was, taught not to put garbage on the floor, asked his Grandpa why he did it. Scob's answer was, "I didn't."

That was it! That was the liar's behavior that had warped my mind as a child. I almost began to hyperventilate, but held it together. My instinct was to get my children away from them as fast as I could so my parents could not screw with their minds as they had with mine. I managed to make it through the week with them without condemnation or accusations. It seemed like such a small thing, denying having thrown a straw paper on the floor, but it was confirmation of all the lies that stripped me of believing what I saw with my own eyes to be real, and taught me to doubt myself. The impact Margaret had on my life was profound, and I hold her close to my heart to this day. She represents the safe haven *Home* is supposed to be.

HOME

The beach
Muir
I was not born there
Yet, it is where
Mother
Gave birth to my soul.

I came
Mind muddied
Shallow murky swamp water
Unaware of the questions to ask
Afraid of the answers
Lost at sea
Who I could be
Riding high on the waves
Who I had become
Crashing against the shore
Washing out to sea in the undertow.

My being unraveled,
Took on many forms.
My parents regressed into
Children, then teens, then
Adults married with children.
I must know them
To know myself.

Each day
As I ran alone beside the ocean
My thoughts,
With the tide
Would ebb and flow.
My tears,
Overflowing turmoil
Ran down my cheek off my chin
Disappeared in the sand
Salt to salt.

Anemones
Attached to one rock
For life, taught me
Treasure my freedom
Accept my singularity
Lest I lose myself
Within another.
The shore renewed
With each breaking wave,
Taught me
Treasure my dear ones
Accept commitment
Lest they slip
Through my fingers
Like grains of sand.

Each day
As I sat alone on the rocks,
The sea gave itself to me.
Raging, roiling power
To use with caution.
Surging strength
To emerge from within.
Silent stillness
To find inner peace.
Caressing, cradling softness
The essence of life
To love.

It is interesting to me now, as I think about the writing exercises I did while at Muir Beach. One was to describe my parents and their lives before I was born in an effort to understand myself through understanding them, seeing them as ordinary people rather than as my parents. I was detailed and of course used my imagination to make up their story, but I thought a lot of it was probably true and it gave me a framework within which I could understand how I came to be. As it turns out, it would have taken much more creativity to even come close to the truth about them. I doubt that pre-marital sex would have entered my mind, let alone the pregnancy scandal, the adoption, the fictitious wedding date. No, I would not have imagined James Thomas, the shadow that lurked even in darkness, from which our distorted family dynamic emerged. Nearly 25 years later, I sat waiting for my first appointment with a woman I had never met not knowing what to expect, but open to possibilities. *Healers* and *Eye of the Storm* express my willingness to let go of my pride and ego, give up my old inaccurate perceptions of myself, and open to life's possibilities.

HEALERS

Dead-end
Sterile
Half-paneled hallway
Single chair
Awaits next patient.
Calmly I wait.

How many sat before me,
Minds disturbed,
Spirits disheartened,
Weighted with deep depression
Dreams forgotten, future disillusioned?
Where are they now?
Healed and healthy?
Happy and whole?

A lifetime ago
I waited
Outside Margaret's office
Life in turmoil
Marriage broken
Speeding
Toward a breakdown.

I sit now
Older wiser
Half-crane, half-owl
No angst stirring my bosom
No crisis churning my guts.
I sit
No longer broken in dire need.
Someone else should
Fill this chair.

Nagging knee pain
Keeps me from
Moving forward
Pride and ego prevented me from
Owning this chair.
Ego in check
I ask for help.
Even Dante had a guide.

EYE OF THE STORM

Life, my life
Cycles
Birth death
Search within without
Self-imposed change
Cast upon me
Ideals gripped so tightly
My hand opens
Only dust remains.
Gently,
I blow it
Back to the universe.

Old perceptions swirl,
Personal hurricane spinning around me
I am the eye,
My past like Ebenezer's ghost
Sucked in
Whirling with me.

Reach deep
Head heart guts
I fear spinning
Out of control.

Ethereal voice,
Let it go
Let it twist and turn
Past has no power
No more power
Over me.

Suddenly,
Storm passes
I fall to the ground
Surrounded by calm
Deafening eerie silence.
My eyes open
World around unchanged, yet
Appears different.
I stand
Brush off debris of a previous life
Walk forward
Joy in my gait
Truth on my lips.

M y knee still hurt like hell and I obviously had more work to
do to heal. Sarno calls the condition Tension Myoneural
Syndrome, or TMS. As he explains it, what happens physically is that the unconscious mind targets a muscle, a nerve, or a
tendon. Then it reduces the oxygen supply to the targeted tissue,
maybe just five percent, but that's enough to cause excruciating
pain. Once stricken with pain, we immediately search for the cause,
so we can make it go away. The mind dredges up memories of old
injuries to the area, of the skiing fall I had eight years before, of
that heavy box I carried yesterday, of the article I read about how
the constant pounding of running on pavement is damaging to knee
tissue.

Understanding how the brain works and is manipulating us is
the primary concept Sarno tries to get across to his readers and

patients. I spent four months following the treatment plan outlined
in Sarno's book, which is basically — make a list of all the things that
may be contributing to your inner rage and write about each item
on the list. The pain was a constant reminder of the concept and
eased now and again to keep me from giving up. Anger from infancy and childhood, like neglect or being treated harshly by parents,
should be included even though it may seem ridiculous. Severe
parental abuse is not a prerequisite for accumulating rage, but will
always be a factor, and can result in what psychoanalysts call narcissistic rage. Perfectionism and "goodism," Sarno's term for striving to
be good, are big offenders, as are workaholism, feelings of inferiori-
ty and low self-esteem. Caretaking and people pleasing can also
generate furious feelings that get repressed. Life pressures and
responsibility and even aging can enrage our unconscious even
though we consciously rationalize and accept our lot. Consciously
suppressed anger accumulates and increases the repressed rage, and
should be added to the list. The most important suggestion was to
"Think the unthinkable." The things that we think we have dealt
with or that seem so childish need to be included. According to
Sarno, the unconscious mind is timeless, so the fact that we are adults
and should be over our childhood traumas is irrelevant. The rule of
thumb is, if you wonder about something, put it on the list.

At first, I stared at my blank page. I'm a reasonably happy person. I have a good life and I am blessed with children, grandchildren, friends and family. I have a wonderful, loving husband who is
my best friend. I don't really hate anyone anymore. I have also
come to know that my parents loved me and did the best they could
raising me and my sister. I love my parents, always have. I actually
felt guilty writing things down. How ungrateful of me to complain
when I have so much to be thankful for. How childish, how 70s, to
put my parents on the list. I'm a grown woman with grandchildren,
isn't it time I was over blaming my parents? Get over it!

As I added to my list, I realized what *think the unthinkable* meant.
Even though I don't consciously feel anger or rage at anyone or over
any particular situation, it may be there buried deeply. Even though
I thought I had dealt with parental issues along the way, I put Mom

and Dad on the list. I had dealt with them while at Muir Beach when I was 27 and divorcing, but since I had only recently discovered the whole *brother* fiasco, I felt justified adding them, but not anxious to reopen those wounds.

So, I made my list as the good conscientious patient Mother taught me to be, including everything I could think of, much of which made me feel small as I wrote it down, my pride flaring up as usual, hot on my neck. I traced back through my memories, my childhood, grade school, high school, old friends and boy friends, work situations, my first marriage, my kids, my sister. All the usual suspects were accounted for. It didn't take long for me to realize that there was a lot of rage I had pushed deep down inside me because to talk about it or be bothered by it seemed weak, petty, and despicable, not to mention, painful. I was determined to get my life back though, get my knee back, so I just started writing. Surprisingly, I had a lot to say.

Avoiding the parent issue entirely for the time being, I focused on my teens. In 1959, my family moved from Michigan to Phoenix, Arizona and I enrolled in 2nd grade at Andalucia Elementary School. From the age of 7 through most of 8th grade I had the same group of girl friends. We were smart, at the head of our class, and were the elite, the teachers' pets. We were ridiculously snobby and called ourselves the *Big Four*. One of the girls had two older sisters who were overweight and unattractive. They were, I suppose, living vicariously through us by trying to tell us how to act, dress, and wear our hair. It made no sense to me, plus I had no interest in kowtowing to anyone. I had my own big sister anyway, who didn't tell me what to do.

One day out of the blue, my three friends each gave me a letter, one worse than the last, trashing me, every part of me – my personality, my family, my looks, my hair. Everything! I was devastated. And angry. I don't remember talking to anyone about it, except Mom, who encouraged me to ignore them and find new friends. It never occurred to me to look at my behavior or actions. My ego and arrogance left no room for self-examination. I began hanging out with the B-team. Nice enough kids. In fact, once I got over my embarrassment and humiliation of being dumped and my discomfort of being the outsider, I started having a lot more fun and a lot more trouble with my new *Friends*.

FRIENDS

In-crowd ousted
Big 4 now 3.
Submit I would not
Ugly older sisters'
Vicarious meddling remakings.

Suddenly friendless,
B-team welcomed
This rejectee.
I learned quickly
Previous snobbery
Hot shot elitism
Prudish pastimes
Missed life's essence.

Street-smart new friends
Earthy
World wise
Exciting but unfamiliar.
Determined to fit in
Risks must be taken
Demon gin smoothed transition.

My new girl friends also had boyfriends, an element I had been a stranger to up to that point. Debbie, my new chum had been dating a boy named Alan. He was older and she had a reputation. I was fascinated and at the same time ill at ease with the boyfriend concept. I was always a bit of a tomboy and never liked all the girly-girly coy stuff. I would usually side with the boys rather than ridicule them with other girls.

Debbie and Alan broke up and he became extra friendly toward me. Needless to say, I was both thrilled and apprehensive having never had a boyfriend before, and he was so suave and flirty. My excitement was soon dampened and my apprehension proved well founded. Alan turned out to be an arrogant and cavalier teenaged womanizer, but I learned that too late. My innocence and discomfort was soon crushed out, replaced by booze with boy chasers. *First Kiss, Redemption,* and *Sleepover* tell the story.

FIRST KISS

Three years my senior
Experienced
Lurid tales past loves
Well known.
He and Debbie
My new friend
An item no longer.

Tall Mick Jagger look-alike
Interested in
Me?
Flattered
Excited
Hand-in-hand walking home
Brady Bunch sweet.

Standing
Talking
My back against Dad's
Mint-green Falcon,
His forearm leaning on the car roof
Facing, he bent
Kissed me
Immediately he knew
It was my first.

So inept
So clumsy
Humiliation and shame
Surged up my back,
Washed over my shoulders,
Flushed my neck
A rising tide of thick embarrassment
Engulfed me.
He said he'd call.
He'll never call.

REDEMPTION

Call he did.
Wants to see
Me?
Parents gone
Come over, small party.
Of course!
Redemption.
A chance for
Sweet redemption.

Walking
Thinking
Better kisser I'll be
This time.
Emotions mixed
Heart over-beating
Apprehensive
Anxious
Excited
Eager to please,
My family role.

His house dimly lit.
Smiling Alan welcomed me in
Necking couch couple
Looked up
Surprised to see *me*.
Distantly familiar
Introductions unnecessary
Party of four feels suddenly uncomfortable
Unfamiliar under-current
Evokes fear.

Pulled by the hand
Into his room,
"We'll give them some privacy."
A good friend he.
Shoulder angel urged,
"Go now. Leave!"
Devil counterpart insisted,
"Stay!"

My mind, fear clouded
Jumbled thoughts bounced.
Go and relive
Embarrassment
Humility,
Stay and
And what?
And maybe
He'll like me.

Insecurity trapped
Reality unaware
Unable to leave.
Paralyzing fear
Blinded my conscience
I could not make him
Stop.

Shaking,
Shorts on backward
Mis-buttoned blouse,
I ran.
From bedroom
Through living room
Past neckers
Out the front door.
I ran.

Heat rose from the blacktop
Fires of Hell nipping my
Rubber-thonged feet
In horrified confusion
I ran.

My neighborhood streets
Eerily unfamiliar
Knowing eyes peering through
Lifted blind slats
Home
I ran.

Crying
Hurting
Bleeding
Sickened
I ran
From him
From myself.

Shame like a shadow
Hung at my back
I could not outrun
What I had become.

SLEEPOVER

Double sleepover
New friend Gina's neat trick.
Two girls
Beefeater gin only chaperone
Walked neighborhood 'til dawn
Silly schoolgirl rebellion.

Stopovers well known
Widower with sons
Drop-ins welcome
Shoot pool
Shoot the breeze
Move on.

Single mother teen hangout
No action.
Walk, talk, drink.
After midnight
Meet Mick and friend.
Memory, judgment booze deadened
Inspired night out
Becomes Mick's backyard camp out.

Powerful lessons learned
Pride swallowed
Shame washed down easily
With gin chaser,
Distilled
Self-delusional excuses.

During that same time, the summer of 1966, old friends of my parents came for a visit. Chris had a big farm with oil wells in Michigan and was probably a father figure to my dad, being at least twenty years his senior. His wife Toot was a kind but rather rigid woman. They had no children. They knew me since my birth and were like grandparents to me and my sister. My memories of farm visits are faint, but fond. Hearty family meals at the big pine dining table always included fresh baked bread or biscuits and home made apple or cherry pie. Diane and I went for tractor rides on the farm and played in the corn silos. It had been 6 years since we had seen them, and it was a small joyous reunion of dear old friends. I had given up my room so they had some privacy and I happily slept on the couch. Since both my grandfathers had died before I was born, Chris was the Grandpa I held in my mind. In one twisted moment described in *Trust*, the relationship was smashed, never to be revived.

TRUST

Chris
Old Michigan landowner
Daddy's boyhood father figure
Farmer
Oil baron
Black gold
Oozing up through corn rows.

Denim overalls
Chris' uniform
Working fields
Socializing
Cash Cadillac buying.

Toot
Childless farm wife
Stoic farm-hand feeder
Cooking dawn to dusk
Ranch house dinner bell ringer.

Fond farm memories
Tractor rides
Silo hide and seek.
Childhood ritual horsy rides
Atop Chris' knee,
Clip-clop clip-clop
T'gallop t'gallop t'gallop.
"Be good or I'll pin
Your ears back!"
Traditional friendly threat
Pseudo step-grandfather.

Family move
Grand Rapids to Phoenix
Birthday, Christmas cards
Kept friendships alive.
Retired farm couple's
First airplane trip
Reunited old friends
Mom and Dad longing
Solid relationships
From another life
Thrilled to see familiar faces.

Chris sat bed's edge
Reminiscing,
How I'd grown
Was I really 13?
He pulled me over
Sat me on his knee.
"Give old Chris
A kiss, for old times."
Childishly innocent
I puckered up.

He shoved his tongue
In my mouth.
Confused
Shaken
Reviled
I pulled away
Ran from the room.
Spitting
Could not change
What was
Lifetime fondness
Instantly vanished.

Sullied wariness
Hung between us
Thick
Heavy
Like humid air
Sprinkled with dirt
Tinged with guilt.

My eyes never met his
Again.
Years later,
When I heard of his death
I was not sad
Nor sorry.

G rateful that the summer was over, I gladly entered high school. It was a big school with about 4000 kids, a good place to meet new faces but equally a place to get lost in and feel alone. The loss of my best friends was still an open wound as was my hard knock summer of too many life lessons. I was happy to be obscure and focused on my work. My new crowd included some sopho- mores and juniors, and I met a sweet guy named Tom. He lived in my neighborhood, but he had not attended my elementary school. It was a clear cut case of puppy love, heart throbs on sight, walking around at lunchtime holding hands. After what I had been through in the summer, you'd think I would be a bit hardened on the whole scene, but part of my nature was being the eternal optimist, or per- haps being in denial. It served me well, but often allowed me to escape reality. Perhaps I watched too much Brady Bunch or Father Knows Best, because I was still pretty naïve. At any rate, this boy- friend-girlfriend thing with Tom seemed exactly how things should be. Even at my young age, it didn't take long for my recent past to catch up with me and Tom dropped my like a rock. The shame burned deep within me, and I grieved for my loss, more for what I had thoughtlessly given away, than for what was taken from me.

I ran into him again at my friend Sarah's house on a Friday night. The whole gang would meet up there to hang out, carouse, and drink. I learned that once I had drunk enough, I didn't feel the searing shame. Friday nights at Sarah's became a regular event. Tom and I would start out disdaining each other, cursing and dismissing. As my mind softened with booze, so did my heart and my inhibitions. Afterward, no matter how much I drank, I always felt like *Damaged Goods*.

DAMAGED GOODS

Nightmares of summer behind me
High school new life ahead
Opportunity abounds.
Fresh faces
Fresh outlook
Past mistakes deeply hidden.

Boyfriend
Every good girl's dream
Cute, kind,
He really likes me.
Between class locker meetings,
Café lunches,
Quad walks.
Dreamy *Teen* magazine love story.

Then nothing
Unanswered calls
Sneers
Snubs
Cold shoulder treatment
Eyes flashed anger and betrayal.

Summer neighborhood news made
High school headlines
Sweet girl-next-door
Bubble bursts
Cannot escape cruel truth.
No penance could forgive this sin
Relieve this shame
He really liked me.
He hates me.

Friday night chance meeting
Friend's free-for-all
Drunken brawl
Becomes weekly tradition
21-year-olds buy
Teens drink.
He insists.
I pretend
He really likes me.
After enough booze
I believe
He really likes me.

Anything wonderful that occurred in my teens was overshadowed by the events of 1966. I learned to chuck my pain, my feelings of shame and self-disgust down deep where even I would not find them. Digging them out in an effort to heal my knee proved to heal my heart and head as well.

CHAPTER FOUR

Exhuming My Ex-Husband's Ghost

I have a labyrinth in my yard. It is out past the split rail fence in an open field. Before my mother died, I had heard of labyrinths, but like most people, I had never seen one and thought it was a maze. The word produces a vision of Jack Nicholson in the height of madness, chasing his young son through a hedge maze in the dead of winter in the movie *The Shining*. This labyrinth is much different than that. It's flat, made of paver stones and sits in the meadow surrounded by nature. Why a labyrinth, you might ask, which a few years ago, I would have asked as well.

Once when I was in San Francisco with my cousin Beverly, she suggested we go over to Grace Cathedral and walk the labyrinth, explaining that it was a spiritual walking path and insisting that I would enjoy it. We didn't make it there at that time, but a few months after my mother died, I was in San Francisco with Phil prior to a business conference. We stayed on Nob Hill and Grace Cathedral was across the street. I felt drawn by it and suggested we go check out this labyrinth.

There are actually two Grace Cathedral labyrinths. The one outside is made of travertine and as you walk it in the morning or early evening you can see the city alive all around you through hanging fog. The other one is inside the cathedral, a grey and purple hand made rug patterned after the ancient European labyrinths.

There are pillars to the right of the labyrinth with photos of the 13th century Chartres Cathedral Labyrinth in France and a brief description of its history. On one pillar the three phases of the walk were written: Purgation or shedding on the walk in — basically letting go of the daily pressures, the weight of the world that hangs on our shoulders; Illumination in the center — opening to life, nature, the universe, the Divine; and Unity or merging on the walk out — returning to the world with grace and sharing the gifts you received.

Perhaps because I had recently lost both of my parents and perhaps because I had begun to question the path I had been walking for years, I was in a vulnerable state. Perhaps it was also because I was in San Francisco, the city which holds so much joy and pain for me, the place of my sons' births and their father's death. Whatever the reason, as I began reading the description of the three phases, my eyes filled with tears and I began to quietly sob. There was sacred music playing softly in the background and the lights were dim, the sun shining in through stained glass windows. I took off my shoes, and stepped onto the path. My tears just kept flowing and my body was convulsing as I walked and wept openly. Once in the center, I sat down, put my forehead on my knees and just gave in to the sadness. I felt as if I could have cried for weeks. I got up after a few minutes and walked the path back out. Phil had patiently waited for me, confused, concerned, and compassionate. Walking out into the fresh cool air, I felt an enormous release. I regained my composure and Phil and I went walking around the city that I love.

About eighteen months later, I decided to build a labyrinth out in the field beyond our yard. My motivation was two-fold. First, I could walk it whenever I wanted, and second, walking the labyrinth was being incorporated into a personal development seminar I was creating with two business colleagues. They had walked with me at Grace Cathedral during the week of that business trip in San Francisco, and were also moved by the experience. The seminars were to be held in our outdoor office so the labyrinth walk would flow beautifully.

In the summer of 2002, I gathered a couple of design experts from Saint Louis and Chicago and a lot of family and friend laborers. In ten days (and ten nights), a replica of the Chartres Labyrinth emerged. Constructed of paver stones, each laid by hand, it was a group effort of sweat, toil and love. The labyrinth is a meditative place, and I walk it often to clear my mind, asking for clarity, inspiration, and guidance. Usually when I walk, thoughts drift in from another place and shift into consciousness. Mom's ashes are mixed in the base layer of stone dust and sand. I find it easy to speak to her there in the open field, long grasses shifting in the breeze, birds and insects chirping, knowing the remnants of her earthly form are beneath me. During many contemplative walks on the labyrinth my mind would become engulfed with thoughts and visions. *Metaphors* and *Fishing* emerged from walks during this time of digging through the mire of my past.

METAPHORS

Metaphors,
Windows
Others peer through,
Gain perspective,
Glimpse
Our inmost thoughts
Fears.

Metaphors,
Mirrors
Reflect back
Our true nature
Dare we look.
Frequently fearsome
We turn away.

Metaphors,
Disguise reality,
Create personal Babel Towers
Designed to keep others
Out,
Instead
Lock us in.

FISHING

Memories
Fish,
Fishing,
Pastime shared
Me and my dad
My boys and me
Tangents yet another time.

Bread, fishes
Brought forth
Blessed
Multiplied
Miraculously fed masses.

Behind scene never mentioned.
Lives surrendered
Gullets slit, gutted
Flesh cleansed
Toxins rid.
Only then
Blessed by God
Only then
Useful to humanity.

I too
Must follow
Fishes fate
Slit my gullet
Fillet my heart
Spit out fine, invisible bones
Lest they get caught in my throat
Choke me
Silence my voice.

Only then
Blessed by God
Only then
Useful to humanity.

The list I had written of possible causes of unconscious rage was on my night table and called to me daily as my knee continued to plague me with pain. Two major topics I had purposefully ignored and side-stepped were my parents and my ex-husband. They were all three dead. There was deep guilt, pain, and sorrow associated with each of them and as I discovered, a fair amount of resentment as well. In order of death I addressed them, my memories of them, of me with them. I spoke to their ghosts and they spoke to me. The story starts when I was 17 and continues for 30 years.

Ron and I met at The Seared Steer, a restaurant in west Phoenix. The Seared Steer was a small chain run by Bernard Lee, a short, cigar-smoking Chinese entrepreneur who liked women. I recall being shocked seeing him with one of his female store managers, knowing he was married with children. I had never seen infidelity blatant and up close before. The restaurant's fare was limited to steaks and burgers, baked potatoes and garlic toast. Bernie packaged his own cheap beef cuts soaked in MSG to tenderize them. He packed them on cafeteria trays out behind his Tempe store in the Arizona heat, flies buzzing. He froze them and delivered them to his other six restaurants once a week. T-bones and burgers, the only meat that didn't give me diarrhea he bought from a local meat packer. As I look back at it now and visualize the scene, the term seedy comes to mind. I see a truck-stop restaurant at a main artery, three-way intersection with waitresses in mini skirts with polka-dot bloomers underneath, an outfit Bernie especially liked. I didn't see it that way then. I was seventeen and full of myself.

I had a boyfriend, Joe, who had just asked me to marry him as he enlisted in the service to avoid the draft, and was shipping out. It was 1969, the Vietnam War was raging, and I was finishing my last semester in high school. The scene was a time warp, a flashback to a previous generation and World War II. My parents, having lived through that era thought this was normal and encouraged my acceptance. It was sudden and unexpected, but seemed like the logical next step, so I said yes. I needed a job to contribute to our future plans. I swore I would not be a waitress because I thought it was demeaning, but I couldn't find work anywhere else since I wasn't eighteen. Ron was the manager of the Seared Steer restaurant, and interviewed me. After applying and having been turned down for a dozen other jobs, I gladly accepted this one. It was a decision that drastically changed the course of my life.

Joe was sent to Fort Ord for boot camp, and was gone for six months. Absence did not make this heart grow fonder, and I became disillusioned with my military beau. I was attending high school from 6 am to 11, and working split sessions from 11:30-2 and 5-9, as well as all day Saturday and Sunday. Joe would call me on Sunday at 6 am, my only day to sleep in. He expected me to go spend time with his mom whom I didn't know well or like, and whom he had not spent ten minutes talking to in over five years. I also had this boss who liked me, whom I found intriguing, charming and worldly. He also was there every day and we had established a fun working relationship. Eventually I called off the engagement and broke up with Joe when he came home on leave.

Ron and I began dating sometime after that. I seemed to be attracted to men who were not like me. Joe was Mexican. Ron was Chinese. My B-team friends were a diverse group of Whites, Mexicans, and Blacks. Maybe I was intrigued by the difference,

although I don't remember focusing on it. Perhaps what was missing for me was a sense of strong cultural tradition which seemed to
be lacking in Arizona and in my family. My parents had not object-
ed to our inter-racial relationship. I don't think they knew any
Chinese families, so had no basis for discrimination against them.

The window into the Phoenix Chinese community opened up
a world I had never known existed. Unlike my parents and my
friends' parents who worked for others, the Chinese in Phoenix
owned a good share of the real estate and businesses in the city.
Having emigrated a generation before, they had created a strong
financial and social base. I spent time in parts of Phoenix and
Scottsdale where money flowed easily, and Ron knew the owner of
every store and restaurant we went into. We dated for about 18
months, and I had thought he was 21 when I met him. Our relationship had already grown pretty serious when I found out he was
not 4 years older than I, but 14. It was a shock, but by that time I
was in love and too naïve to consider the lie a breach of trust or the
age difference a concern. I see it now as the first breach of many,
described in *Initial Deceit*.

I N I T I A L   D E C E I T

Seventeen
Jobless
Engaged
High-school senior
Hired by my
Future husband.

World-wise, suave, exotic
Multi-plumed toucan
Spoke my language in a new dialect
Opened my eyes to wonder.
Charismatic Asian charmer
Coaxed this entranced cobra
From my closed basket
Made me dance to his tune.

Love
Bridged age chasm between us
Generation gap looked
Sidewalk crack thin
Through naïve astigmatism.

My relationship with Ron was kept a secret from his parents. His mother was adamantly against the thought of her children marrying outside the race. Ron had had a long-term relationship with a local Chinese woman from a good family, who worked as a stewardess. He let his parents go on believing they were still connected. She was living in San Francisco since that was her airline's hub. When she came to town, Ron would see her and take her around the family as usual, which I stupidly and willingly went along with. I recall going with him to buy theater tickets for them. His sister knew of our relationship, and was kind and welcoming to me, but also kept it quiet from the family. I completely denied that this deception bothered me. I tried to be so understanding, yet I felt ashamed like a mistress or other woman, when in fact, I was his real girlfriend. I was also hurt that Ron was accepted by my family, was good enough for me, but I was not good enough for him. His perpetuation of this old relationship, a ruse played out for his parents, was a bad sign that I was too young and blind to interpret.

I had become the manager of the Phoenix restaurant and Ron went to California to open two new locations in Fullerton. He wrote me three letters during the four months he was away. His best friend Jack would come by the restaurant and look out for me especially during late closing hours. I remember him telling me that he had never seen Ron as taken with anyone as he was with me. I was thrilled, of course. When Ron returned, we picked up exactly where we left off. Not long after, I was cleaning his apartment and saw a torn up letter in the waste basket. Being snoopy and suspicious, I pieced it back together and read it. It was from a woman he obviously had an intimate relationship with while in Fullerton. I was heart-broken and did not know what to do. After hours of crying, my guts twisted, I finally confronted him. He talked his way out of it, but my trust was shaken. Being young and desperately wanting or needing to be loved, I quickly recovered and put that episode behind me and out of my mind. We were together and that was all that mattered.

Ron became fed up with Bernie and his restaurants and he and I decided to apply to a local technical college. I quit the Seared Steer and worked nights at General Electric as a keypunch operator while I attended school. Ron quit work altogether, living off his GI Bill. We were a couple, comfortable and happy together. I lived at home, he lived with Jack. We didn't have much but it didn't matter. I remember the carefree feeling of those days in *Less Was More*.

LESS WAS MORE

Innocent
Free
In love.
Hand-in-hand skipping
Down Jefferson Street
South Phoenix
Urban college campus in sight
First GI Bill check in hand.

Feeling flush
Laughing
Singing
"We're in the money."

Times were not
All bad.

Having lived nearly twice as long as I had, Ron had already served in the Air Force and gotten out on a medical discharge. He had enlisted at 17. In less than 2 years he had a near fatal emergency. An internal goiter which was the cause of him losing a tremendous amount of weight began to choke off his windpipe and a tracheotomy was the only thing that saved him. His thyroid had been removed and he took thyroid medication from then on. It is no wonder I looked at him as worldly and wise. His life experience was doubly as rich as mine. I was just a kid who wanted nothing more than to get away from my parents and their control. At the end of our first year of school, Ron and I made a plan to move to San Francisco and live together. It was 1971, the time of peace, free love, flower children and shacking up. My parents saw it differently, described in *Ball and Chain,* which set the tone for our marriage and life together.

BALL & CHAIN

Run off to San Francisco
Live together.
Live in sin
According to Mom.
On breaking the news
I entered a nightmare
More disturbing than Alice's
Fall down the rabbit hole.
I learned what Mother thought
Of me.
I didn't know then
Or for years,
It was what she thought
Of herself.

The Queen of Spades chased me
Screaming
"Are you crazy?
You're so stupid!
If you go live with him
He'll leave you.
He'll never marry you.
You'll be left there
Alone.
If he loved you he'd marry you.
You're just a slut."

Playing-card soldiers closed in on me
As my mind ran in circles
Hysterically looking for the
Keyhole to escape through.

I had not expected
Such anger or outrage
Stripped of all self-worth
Complete demoralization, shame
Engulfed me.
Is this how parents say,
"We love you.
We're worried about you.
We'll miss you.
We want the best for you?"
At 19,
I didn't know how
To translate.

Witness to this tragic scene was
The man I loved.
Ashamed
Confused,
Sobbing, sobbing
He held me
In his arms.
My tears
Did not wash away
Humiliation.
Now he knew my
Worthlessness
He saw the child I was
Not the woman he wanted.

Saving the day, the hero,
Dark knight on white steed
Said we'd get married
He'd rather marry me
Than lose me.
It was dramatic
But was this love?
At the time it did not matter
Perhaps it kept me from knowing
What was truly in his heart.
Taught by Marian and Scob
Leave sleeping dogs lie,
We never spoke of it
Again.

N ow that we had agreed to marry before just picking up and
moving to San Francisco, the issue of where to get married
became the big question. I had left the Catholic Church a few
years earlier and had no desire to return. Ron was a member of the
First Chinese Southern Baptist Church of Phoenix, but had also
rejected his religious traditions. Anyway, his mother who remained
against the union forbade a ceremony in her church that would
embarrass her in front of her friends and her god. Freed from religious constraints, we decided to marry in Las Vegas on the way to
San Francisco. The union took place in the *Chapel of the Bells*. Yes,
the very same chapel that years later appeared in the movie,
Honeymoon In Vegas.

Chapel of the Bells

Soon to be Mother-in-law
Agreed
I was not good enough
For her son
Refused to participate
In sacred union.
Churchless, we chose
Las Vegas wedding venue
Chapel of the Bells.
Preacher in shades
Me in hot pants and boots
Family looking on
How normal it all seemed.
Ethereal, bizarre
It seems now.

Where did I come from
That this
Marriage mockery
Was acceptable?
Little did I know
Cross-border secret marriage
Justice of the Peace presiding
Was hereditary.

Did I marry for love? Or
Was I running away?
Tyrant father
Sickly, demanding mother
Hotter than Hell Arizona
Past I was ashamed of
Family drama I was sick of.

> I did not know
> I was running to me,
> I did not know where
> I would be found.

Looking at old wedding photos, I can laugh at myself today. I still wonder what we were all thinking, me in my crushed green velvet hot pants and black boots, hair down to my waist; the preacher in sun glasses; both our families standing with us as if we were in a stained-glass cathedral. The normalcy of it astounds me. I was watching *Honeymoon In Vegas* with my son Darin one evening years ago, and when I saw the wedding scene I said, "Hey, Darin, that's where Daddy and I got married!" To which he responded adamantly, "You did not!" His reaction only confirmed the strangeness of it all.

What is saddest is that the seriousness of marriage itself, the joining of two people in a sacred bond was lost somewhere between the drama scene with my parents and that Las Vegas chapel. Perhaps that is what allowed me to leave in the end, the lack of profound connection and the thought that it never meant that much in the first place. Running away from my parents transferred to running away from Ron. It took years for me to understand that I was running from myself and ultimately to myself. *I Left My Heart* describes the impact that my mother's words and her curse had on me. In the end, I had to take care of myself. *Little Rosie* is the vision of finally realizing that.

I LEFT MY HEART

Life began anew
Clay Street, San Francisco.
I missed them
My hurtful parents
First time
Away from home
A home that was mine
No longer.

Had Mom any idea how deeply
She scarred me?
She had no idea.
Legacy of verbal abuse
Passed from her father
Through her
To me.
Like an over sharp knife
The cut so clean
Pain isn't felt until the blood
Begins to flow.

Tables turned
Fate jumped the track
Years later
I was the one who left.
Perhaps I never believed
He loved me.
Perhaps I never believed
I was good enough.
It didn't matter
After all, I was there
Alone
As Mother predicted.

LITTLE ROSIE

Shhhh,
It's ok don't be afraid.
I'm here
I've got you
I'll protect you.

Shhhh,
Let me hold you
Put your head on my shoulder
Relax as I sway
To and fro
To and fro.

Like Superman
I will swoop down
From above
Scoop you up
Whisk you away
From danger
From pain.

Cradling you in my arms
I will take you high
In the sky
Through billowy clouds
To sunlight
To safety.

Like the wind I will run
Harder
Faster
Barely touching ground
Herd of wild stallions
Pacing me
Closer
Closer
All fear gone
As I run
Into my own open arms.

Ron and I stayed married for over seven years. I often think that Ron saved me from a horrible trailer park life with some loser out in the desert. Maybe he did. Mom and Dad lived in a trailer before — it could have been contagious, hereditary even. I had also stopped drinking when I began dating Ron, which was a definite benefit for my sanity, health and well-being. Asians often have a physical aversion to alcohol. Ron told me he had tried to drink in the Air Force but he would always pass out, so he gave up trying. I gave him Nyquil once for a cold, and he turned red as a lobster from head to toe and began slurring his words. As I helped him to the bathroom he passed out cold, knocking me to the floor, his foot in the waste basket. I never wanted him to know how awful I could be when I drank, so I decided to quit since we would never drink together.

Living and working in San Francisco certainly provided broader horizons than Phoenix. It was The City! It was both beautiful and intriguing to this little girl from Arizona. Our apartment was small but fine and life was good. I worked for an international shipping and mining company downtown and Ron worked for an airfreight forwarder. Neither of us made much money, but it didn't seem to matter.

We both completed our undergraduate degrees at Golden Gate University night school, something Ron encouraged me to do for which I am grateful. I believe he saw in me a spirit and potential

that I felt within, but which was not consciously visible to me for
many years. I was pregnant as my final semester came to a close. I
didn't walk with my class at graduation since my life was moving
way beyond classrooms and college.

Dennis' birth marked my entrée into adulthood. I was no
longer a child, I had a child; a little life I held in my hands. From
the time I was diagnosed with IBS, after our hideous Thanksgiving
trip to Phoenix, I changed my attitude, became stronger, and
stopped feeling like a victim. I knew then our marriage was in trouble, I just didn't know what to do about it. I worked part time after
Dennis was six months old and Ron had been laid off from work.
When Dennis was two, Darin was born. I had thought I could never
love anyone as much as Dennis, but I found I was wrong. I loved
them both in a way I never knew existed.

Ron had been laid off again and I was forced to return to work
right away while still nursing Darin. It tortured me to have to leave
my sweet baby. The drive was long and my breasts would leak at
work. It's no wonder I resented Ron's lazy attitude and inability to
hold a job. I had not realized before that I was much more ambi-
tious than Ron, and that he depended on me financially. We went
through cycles of Ron working and being laid off and ultimately he
landed a job with Hughes Air West. It was exciting that we had
flight privileges but Ron never wanted to use them. We could have
flown to Chicago for the weekend, or to Canada or Baja California,
but he was not really interested. Instead we flew to Phoenix to visit
our families, our only vacations. The years Ron and I spent together were not horrible, they were empty. Dennis and Darin filled that
emptiness, but not the void between Ron and me.

I was a computer programmer and worked as a freelance con-
sultant which gave me the freedom I needed to care for the boys. A
girl friend at work was divorcing her husband and we chatted about
it. I was taught never to discuss personal issues like money or family matters so I was intrigued at how open she was about her failed
marriage. For the first time, I became aware that divorce was an
option. It had not occurred to me before. As my resentments
toward Ron grew, the idea of divorce wormed its way into my mind.
The more it wormed, the more I felt I needed out. I was incapable

of seeing my fault in the relationship, I just was not that mature or psychologically astute. He began to take on the face of the enemy and I felt like I had to get away from him to survive. I started drinking again after work with friends on Friday nights and flirting with men at the office. In my mind the relationship was over and I stepped outside of it with someone I worked with. At that point I really hated who I was becoming within the boundaries of our marriage. This is not the woman I perceived myself to be. I didn't even think I was capable of such wrongdoing. I found myself becoming hostile toward Dennis and Darin which really pushed my hand. That is when I decided we must get a divorce. During that discussion, Ron told me that I was everything he ever wanted in woman. I was shocked. Why didn't I know that? I thought he had little love for me, and felt something like resigned disdain. I felt guilty and angry at him for his comment, instead of love and a melted heart. I didn't understand, and at that time, I don't think I wanted to. I had crossed over some invisible line, walked through an energy field to another realm and there was no going back. I wrote *'til Death* with that final, fatal scene in mind.

'TIL DEATH

Love vowed
All the rest of my days
'til death
Do us part.

Never understood
How you loved me
You thought I knew
Didn't think
You had to show it.

Passive by nature
Your affection indifference
Nightly rejection
Taken personally
Seven years
Mirror staring
Never good enough
For you.
I didn't know how to be
The woman you wanted
I didn't know how to be
Me
With you.

Weakened
Disheartened
Becoming hostile
My lovely innocent boys
You became the enemy
I had to get away
My needs
Ripped our sweet family
Apart.

Survival
Life or death.
My life
Your death.

We continued to live together for six months but they were the most strained I can recall. A certain inertia had set in and I think if I had not begun to look for an apartment for Ron, he would have just stayed and we would have continued on like that forever. I had continued seeing this other man which further complicated the situation. When I look back, I see myself as hard and hardhearted although I never thought of myself in those terms. I imagine others did.

When Darin was two, Dennis four, Ron and I divorced without fighting, without anger, without passion, which is how we lived our life together. Our divorce was simple. In fact, most of it was accomplished with a do-it-yourself book, complete with legal forms. We finally used a lawyer, but just one. We had very little property or anything to split up and filed for joint custody. It was California after all. We did everything to make the split easy on the boys. Ron moved nearby and we had them every other day and every other weekend. The movie, *The Squid and the Whale*, had nothing on us.

Hughes Air West was being sold to Republic Airlines. For about a year between the announcement of the sale and the actual event, Ron did nothing about finding another job he just went along and let it happen. Ron was offered a job with Republic on the condition of relocation, so he moved to Minnesota where Republic was headquartered. Perhaps that's what he wanted, or needed. He thought it would be no problem seeing the kids since he still had free flight privileges, but again, he rarely got around to using them. The first summer he was there, he took the boys to Minneapolis for six weeks. They spent days in a fun day care center and had a good visit with their dad.

In the middle of the night before the day he was to bring them home, Ron had a heart attack. My brother-in-law called me around four am with this news. Frantic, not knowing what Dennis and Darin had seen and experienced of this tragedy, I flew there immediately. I cried the entire flight, for him, for the kids and for me. On seeing Ron in ICU, I was overcome with guilt that I had caused him such pain and caused his heart attack. The fact that he smoked and ate red meat with loads of fat was not going to relieve me of my guilt. At first I felt I had to take him back, take him home, nurse him back to health and give up the life I had started making for myself and the boys. Thankfully, I slept on that thought, and the next day I was able to shake off that feeling. I took the boys home and Ron stayed in Minnesota with help from friends. In six months he had returned to work.

Four years later, he moved back to San Francisco and within a year the boys and I moved to New York. He remarried and had another son. Every summer, I would send Dennis and Darin back to San Francisco, actually Oakland then, to spend four to six weeks with Ron and his new family. I thought it was important for them to have a relationship with him even if it was only a few weeks a year. The summer when the boys were 14 and 16 was disastrous — a mix of teenage rebellion and stepmother unreasonableness. Ron allowed his wife to throw Dennis out of the house. The disruption and chaos from 3000 miles away was disturbing and I was glad when they finally returned home. A week and a half later, ten years after his first heart attack, Ron had another, and it was fatal. All Hell broke loose and the boys were devastated.

The guilt I felt when I divorced Ron, and again when he had the first heart attack, returned with a vengeance, engulfing me, ripping me apart. No one I had ever loved had died except my grandmother, and I had been too young to grasp the full impact. My sorrow for the loss Dennis and Darin were suffering was all mixed up with my own sorrow and guilt. I had never dealt with my feelings about our entire relationship. As a result, I had never forgiven myself for breaking up the marriage and I felt I had caused Ron's health problems. For years after whenever I spoke about the situation, the words would choke in my throat and I would well up with tears. I remained overcome with guilt that plagued me until I wrote *Guilt Sentence*.

GUILT SENTENCE

How dare you
Die?
Leave me burdened
Sorrow guilt,
Sadness guilt,
Fear guilt.
Haven't I shouldered
Enough
Guilt?

Divorce
I insisted only way.
Severing umbilical cord
Between father, sons.
First nail
Your coffin.

Self-proclaimed
Unimportant Dad
Unnecessary
Life's scheme
Dealt you out
Boys
Really didn't need you
You moved far away.
Somehow,
All my fault.
Nail two.

Returning our boys
Tomorrow,
Summer visit over
Anxious mother waiting.
Sweet reunion dream
Turned nightmare
Wee hours cardiac arrest.
My boys
My babies
What horrors had their
Innocent eyes seen?

Was the pain so intense
Your heart actually
Broke?

Guilt unbearable
Flash flood rivulet
Eroded my cheeks
Rained down on
Sierra Nevadas
Rockies
Mighty Mississippi.

Lying there
ICU
I saw your grandma
So old, feeble you looked.
Had I
Done this to you?
Third nail.

My lot
Blinded by guilt
Take you back
Take you home
Heal you
Care for you.
Morning light
Cleared mind fog
I could not.
Guilt sentence
Served easier than
Life sentence
With you.

Decade elapsed
California summer
Six week discord
Unreasonable raging
Stepmother.
Dad
Could not
Would not
Stand up for his
Number one son.
Fourth
Final nail.

How dare you
Die?
Leave sons burdened
Lifetime scars
Me
My boys.
Is it all
My fault?
It isn't my fault.

W e all went to California for the funeral. It was an odd family reunion of all my ex-in-laws. It was a scene repeated
numerous times as Ron's dad died a year later and his mother a few years after that. I had maintained relationships with them
all so the boys would know their family. What sticks in my head is
Ron's mother walking up to the casket between Dennis and Darin
and swooning when she got there, screaming that his lips were all
wrong, and how could they have ruined his lips. They calmed her
and helped her to a seat. Even though she was against our union to
begin with, once the boys were born she gave up her dream of
Ron's perfect wife and accepted me, us. I know she loved Dennis
and Darin and was ever grateful to have them in her life.

Dennis slipped a photo in Ron's chest pocket of the three of
them from a happier time. They rode in the hearse with their stepmother and brother. There was a Catholic service since his wife was
Catholic. I sat knowing that would be the first time he would turn
in his grave. He wasn't buried immediately, so before we returned
to New York, Dennis and Darin wanted to see Ron's grave. I took
them to the cemetery and found it closed, the gates chained and
locked. It would not be the last time that Mom and her two sons
staged a break-in. We climbed the fence carefully, not to become
impaled on the pointed filigree posts. I had only the gravesite number, so it took us a while walking among the dead to find Ron's plot.
The grave marker was not yet in place, but at least there was some
kind of closure at seeing the grave. During another trip to
California, I returned to his grave, and kneeling, with art paper and
crayons, made two rubbings of the headstone for Dennis and Darin
to keep. While on my knees, I asked Ron's forgiveness.

CHAPTER FIVE

Who Is This Woman?

From before our divorce until Ron's death, perhaps from my teens, it seems to me I was searching, searching for something that was missing. Freud would say it was lack of love from my dad, since we had little or no relationship, or some deeper neurosis surrounding child-parent affection. Nevertheless, I searched for this missing element in the men that I met and was attracted to. I searched for it in bottles of booze. I would repeat the same scenario over and over again, making bad choices and the same mistakes.

I would never tell men all about me. I knew if they found out, they would leave. Marian's continuing curse of not being desirable, lovable, worthy, or deserving, I had accepted as my fate. So, as I realize now I did with Ron, I would become what I thought someone else wanted me to be. The paradox is that they would soon realize that I wasn't the same person they had been attracted to or fallen in love with in the first place, and they would leave anyway. I gave up myself, bartered my dignity and self respect for false love. It was a vicious cycle that played out time and again and is described in *Crimes Against Humanity*.

CRIMES AGAINST HUMANITY

Road to here
Twisted,
Rocky,
Blind alley groping
Open doors false way out.
Dejavu
Oft repeated vicious circle.

First marriage
Family of origin escape
Father figure 15 years my senior
Good man,
Just not good for me.
Demise
Divorce ensued.

Our children
My sons,
Bright beacons
Mirrors reflecting insightful glimpses
Compass needles pointing
True North.

San Francisco fog
Clouded judgment,
Bargain basement hunting
Searching
Not knowing for what
Seldom looking within
Remaining without.

Unwilling, afraid to see
I could have my dreams
Not aware
I had my own purpose
My own destiny
My own worth.

Adopting another's dreams
Wearing another's glasses
Blurred my vision,
Led me down false paths.
Kept me hidden from myself
And others.

Time after time,
In time,
Crimes against humanity
My humanity
Self-inflicted
Grew unbearable.
I would crack
Ray of light
Ray of hope
Shone through.
Aloneness
Loneliness
Looked appealing.

Time after time,
In time,
Shouting, Enough! I would
Stand up for myself
Walk away
Try again.
Different man
Different dreams
Same cycle
Same pain.

I n my sixteen years as a single mother I had five relationships that followed this same path and ended in disaster. The last of these failed attempts at love and relationship really pushed me over the edge. When it was over, I was physically sick, mentally exhausted, and willing to see my part in these failures.

This last relationship was with a man I worked with, actually worked for, before transferring out of his area. Another of my repeated poor judgments, dating men I worked with, which had started with Ron. No matter how discreet and secretive, or open and aboveboard the relationship is, it carries an element of deceit in the workplace. It has an affect on everyone else it touches and you are subject to everyone's ridicule and disdain. Your business becomes everyone's business. This work/love relationship undermined me in every way, most critically by eroding my inner confidence and credibility. After about two years, the relationship deteriorated into an infrequent tryst followed by mutual remorse. The longer it went on, the more mentally abusive it became for us both and the sicker I got. We were caught in a deadly dance and the music would not stop. I remind myself that I could have stopped it at any time, I just didn't.

I began suffering from severe bouts of colitis that could attack at any moment – walking in New York City after a nice dinner, driving in the car, riding in a carriage in Central Park – anywhere. I tried to change my eating habits to control it, as if what I was eating was causing the problem. A futile attempt at denial. I switched to decaf coffee. Stopped eating beef. Switched from decaf to tea. Stopped drinking tea. No matter what I put in my mouth, it roiled my guts. This physical manifestation I was well acquainted with from my own experience years before and from watching Mom.

I finally had to admit that I had only one choice, to end the relationship completely. I did so, and miraculously, my symptoms ceased. I could breathe. I could relax. I did not realize the level of stress I had been under. I actually felt a release from a physical confinement and a lightness I could not remember feeling before. I felt as though I had allowed myself to be subjected to brain washing by willingly denouncing my own thoughts, ideas, and ideals in favor of his. So he would love me. So he would not leave me. We parted amicably, and continued our working lives in close proximity to each other without animosity or anxiety. When it was over, it was really over, and I felt no emotional pangs in his presence. *Secret Plague* describes the deadly embrace of a bad relationship and the damage done harboring secrets.

SECRET PLAGUE

Lies, deceits
Secret lives
Internal injuries
Slowly ulcerating wounds
Killing
From inside
Out.

Unnoticeable
Hidden
Behind false smiles and half-truths
Festering in the bowels of darkness
Like a plague
Infecting
All
Who breathe the same air.

Pain
Of a horrible truth,
Stabbing
At the telling,
Once told paves way
For forgiveness.
Power of the secret
Gone
Dissipated into nothingness.
The soul lightened
Healing begins.

R on died shortly after that breakup. Being sick of failed relationships and caught in the after shock of Ron's death, a sabbatical from any serious involvement was welcome. I had a date now and then over the next few years, but my heart was not in it. I felt as though if I never had a man in my life again it would be ok with me. I gladly dedicated myself to spending time with Dennis and Darin, who were then 16 and 14.

I love my sons dearly. They are the gifts from our marriage that I cherish every day. I always felt I did what was best for them, that I was a good mother. We grew up together basically, and survived hard, lean times and difficult situations. As I reflected on the years I spent as a single mother, the joy and the stress of it, I couldn't help thinking that as much as I loved them, I had not always made good choices, and some of my choices must have harmed them as much as some of my mother's choices harmed me. I wrote *Mother or Monster II*, and had more compassion for Mom as a result.

MOTHER OR MONSTER II

How does a woman
Divorce her husband
Tear apart
Her lovely family
Because her needs
Were not met?

My marriage was killing me
If I didn't survive
Neither would my children.

How does a woman
Who professes to love
Her children
Leave them
With her boyfriend
For two months
While she works in Asia?

I was sole supporter
Asia offered good money
I called every day.

How does a woman
Leave her children
Home alone
While she works late
Night after night?

I had a big job
Tight deadlines
I called every night.

How does a woman
Leave her children
Home alone
On weekends
To spend time
With a boyfriend?

I couldn't bring my boyfriend
Home to stay
That wouldn't be right
So I went there
And I called.

I don't regret my divorce
I don't regret having worked hard
And long
And far away
I don't regret having a boyfriend.

I regret
Having hurt the ones I love the most.
If they were ever
Lonely because of me
If they were ever
Afraid because of me
If they ever felt less than
Or not good enough
My rantings and ravings
My absence
Speaking louder than words
I am saddened
I am ashamed.

I love my boys — men now
With all my heart
I always have.
I hope they forgive me.
I know they forgive me.
I must forgive myself.

A bout three years later, I started dating Phil, my husband. Unlike other men I had dated who were either peers or managers at work, Phil and I met serving on the board of a nonprofit agency that helps disadvantaged inner city women and their children. I didn't really know too much about Phil, except that he was dedicated to helping others and he seemed to have a good spirit. I asked Phil to a formal company dinner dance in the fall of 1994, and that was the beginning of a new kind of relationship for me. I had decided to try something different, honesty. I also wanted to get to know Phil first, before becoming entangled in physical intimacy. We had dated once a week for about two months when I left for California to attend a group session with my therapist Margaret. It had been planned for a while, and couldn't have been a better time for me to see her. I did not want to make the same mistakes I had made in the past. On the plane, I was thinking about Phil and our relationship, how I felt about him, and where it might go. I wrote *Awakenings* during that flight.

AWAKENING I

They seep
Back into my consciousness
From dormant depths.
Buried by time.
Buried by pain.

I can feel them
Emerging
Slowly.
Beginning to flow
To every nerve
To every cell.

They creep into my mind.
Slowly.
First weekly,
Then daily,
Now hourly.

I try to control them.
Not too fast.
Let them grow.
Slowly.
Enjoy the sensations
Tingling
Flush
Racing heart.

A call
A touch
A kiss
Brings warmth
A smile
An inner glow.

I sigh.
Such joy.
To experience the feelings
Of new love.

AWAKENING II

Fantasy.
Longing.
Desire.
With closed eyes
I feel you.

Your hand on my neck
Pulls me close.
Your eyes
Peer through mine
Into my soul.
You see my nakedness
What I want
What I need.

A powerful embrace.
Your hands
Sear my back.
Your kisses
Burn my neck.
Your body heat
Engulfs me.
At last
Your mouth on mine
Sets me afire.

With closed eyes
I feel you.
All of you.

AWAKENING III

In my reckless youth
Sex came first
Knowing later.
No discipline.
No control.
No restraint.
Instant gratification.

This time
It feels good
Getting to know you.
Talking.
Sharing.
Laughing.
I want to know you.
I like imagining
You and me.

Your kiss is sweet.
Your touch gentle.
Your laugh contagious.
It feels right
Holding your arm
Walking the city streets.
Your call
Warms my heart
Brings a smile to my face.

In time
We will share
Lover's secrets.
In time
We will quench
Each other's thirst.

Right now
I am enjoying you.
Right now
I need
A passionate kiss.

AWAKENING IV

I have fears.
Are you ready
For me?
Can we fall in love
Lose ourselves in each other
Without losing self?
Find ourselves in each other
The hidden treasure
Of love.

Love, a mirror
Opens the door to ourselves.
Are we
Brave enough
To go through the looking glass?
Wise enough
To recognize what we see?
Strong enough
To accept the dark side
Of ourselves?
Of each other?

I am full of love
Bursting with passion
Longing for relationship.
Are you?
We can still
Turn back.
Or can we?

I feel myself being drawn
Towards you.
If you take my hand
My heart will follow.

AWAKENING V

As I fly away from you
I feel
I am flying
Into your arms.

You have occupied my thoughts
These idle hours.
I have told you things
My secrets.
Created a false sense
Of intimacy
Of closeness.
Or have I?

Have I
Drifted into your thoughts?
Have I
Entered your fantasies
Become your desires
As you have mine?
Would you blush
If I knew?

I'll show
You mine
If you'll show
Me yours.

I had adopted the attitude that I am who I am, take me or leave me. Not in a negative or hostile way, but more in an attempt at truth. If Phil didn't like me when he got to know me, really know me, then that was ok and I would move on. When I returned from California, I felt even surer of my decision to just be me and let the cards fall where they may. I mustered the courage and read these poems to Phil. He was surprised and pleased. Phil was on the same wave length about truth and being real with one another and one day handed me two binders of personal writings. I was a bit overwhelmed, but knew then that this relationship was becoming something very special. *Never Say Never*, because you just don't know when the right person will appear on your path.

NEVER SAY NEVER

Better acquainted
Me myself I
World has had its way
With me.
Stronger
Wiser
Willing to try again.

This time
No secrets
Nothing to hide
Nothing to lose
Past
Not regretted
Not repeated.

Standing naked
With my truth
Know me
Take me as I am
Love me as I am
Or leave me
Alone.

Honesty, trust
Fertilizes
Love, intimacy, self
Flourishes.
Well tended garden
Mutual respect
Togetherness
Apartness.

A s my relationship with Phil grew over the next few months, I knew it was different, I was different, and I did not want to screw it up. Here was a man I could be real with, be myself and not fear he would turn and walk away from me. I read his writings and knew a great deal about this man I was coming to love more and more. In sharing my life story with him, a pattern emerged that I was not fully conscious of before, at least not in these stark and obvious terms. When I drank, all bets were off, I had no idea what might result. I could have one drink and go home, or I could have many and black out, ending up in situations that I would otherwise never be in.

I felt my relationship with Phil was my best shot at an open, honest and loving partnership. I traveled a lot on business, hosting conferences, entertaining customers, and we had had some wild times. I could not continue in the same vein and insure I could honor a commitment of love and trust. Since I could not control my behavior once booze passed my lips, it was clear to me I had to stop drinking if I hoped to maintain my relationship with Phil. I had a choice between a loving relationship grounded in honesty, trust, sanity and clarity, and the warmth of that first gulp of gin spreading through my body's sensory network, electrifying every cell. It was always just the first gulp. Every other was a futile attempt to recapture that feeling. Phil did not drink, so I would not be tempted at dinner watching my partner swill down a martini while I sipped sparkling water.

The blue pill or the red pill? For once I chose right and changed my life. I embarked on a journey of self discovery and fulfillment that I could not have imagined, with a whole man eager to meet me at every juncture, be my life partner. In time our families melded into one and together we learned how to walk through tragedy with grace and embrace joy with the glee of a child. We have had plenty of both and I suspect will have plenty more. I wrote *Soul Mate* and *Miracles* for Phil.

SOUL MATE

How do you know
If it's right?
If he's right?
After being wrong?

Standing at his bookshelf
I knew.

Timidly reaching up
Touching them
Fearing they were
My imaginings.
They are my books
I thought,
Knowing they were
His books.

Eerie.
I felt transparent.
Spine after spine
Stared at me
Spoke to me
In a secret familiar tongue.

He has been to the places I've been.
He must speak my language.
Warmth and kinship
Flooded me.

I used to pray
Riding the R train,
"God, give me a sign
A decent man
Reading a good book."

Here was my decent man
Reading *my* good books.

What more did I need?

MIRACLES

With you
I want to welcome birds home
In spring
Smell the world around us
Come to life.

With you
I want to feel summer warmth
Sun shining in windows
Reflecting on the pond.

With you
I want to be blinded
By fall's vibrant colors
Jump into piles of
Raked leaves.

With you
I want to snuggle
By the fire
Watch old man winter
Snow blanket the earth
Walk hand in hand
Through white woods.

For all my life
I have dreamed of you
Prayed for you
Often discouraged
Ever optimistic.
Now at my side
You are more
Than I knew to ask for.

With you
I want to do everything.
With you
I know we can do anything.

M y lies and secrets and hiding past indiscretions only kept people away from me, didn't let anyone in. I came to understand
that in order for anyone to love me, I had to love myself and
be myself. It sounds so simple, but it took me a long time to figure
it out. Who was I, really? What did I stand for? What would I be
willing to die for? The answers to these questions, what I had been
searching for all along were within me. With the love of a very special man, the program of AA, and a commitment to myself of truth
and trust, I was finally on an *Inward Journey*.

INWARD JOURNEY

Inward journey
Uncharted territory
Underground cavern spelunking
Dark, alone
Slow, careful forward advancement
Belly slithering
Primordial ooze.

Crack of light illuminates
Unseen cove, left
Sacred chamber, right
Twenty foot ceiling
Forty foot drop
Shadows on inner walls
Trigger ephemeral sensations, emotions
Physical reactions.

Stalagmites stalactites nearly meet
In the middle
Lifetime deposits
Drip from above
Bubble up from below.
Feeling my way
Dodging jutting rocks
Overhead boulders
Knife-edge sharp corners.

Gradual committed effort
Archeological dig
Reveals
Priceless relics
Ancient heirlooms
Familiar lost shards.

Dawn of man
One man at a time
Each in his own time
We come face to face
Recognize ourselves
Accept ourselves
From the inside out.

W ith Margaret's guidance as a psychotherapist during the time of my divorce, I had walked through my childhood, my relationships with my parents and their relationship, as well as my relationship with Ron. Since I felt I had dealt with him, my parents and all my childhood imprinting, I had not gone to seek help when Ron died. Since we had been divorced for so long at that point, I figured I was fine, and anyway, I was pretty self-sufficient — a synonym for egotistical and prideful it turns out.

When I started writing, I discovered just how much I had kept bottled up and pushed down inside. What I learned as I was writing these poems about Ron, our wedding, our marriage, our divorce and his death, was that I had not fully dealt with my deepest feelings and emotions regarding him, nor my perceptions about myself. This was the cause of my colon issues a quarter of a century earlier, a major cause of my current knee pain and everything in between. It was about time that I got brutally honest with myself and really dug out all of this once and for all to look at it and attempt to understand. Spilling my guts out onto paper was the real beginning of my healing, of recovering the full use of my knee and of being freed from the internal bondage that kept me emotionally locked up, and physically in pain. It has allowed me to not only understand myself better, my motives, my dark side, and my weaknesses, but also through that understanding and acceptance of myself, I began to feel settled and comfortable down to my bones.

CHAPTER SIX

Sacred Origin

I usually saw my parents once or twice a year either at summer-time or during the holidays. They often went to San Jose to get away from the Arizona heat in the summer, and I would go meet them there for a day or so. They rarely came to San Francisco or New York, but I would make the trip to Phoenix. I wouldn't say we were estranged, but we didn't have the kind of relationship where we would talk daily or even weekly. If I called them once a month I thought I was being attentive. They had their own life. For fifteen years from the time they retired, they traveled around in a motor coach six months of the year. In the beginning, they went all over the country and belonged to motor coach organizations like, Thousand Trails, and went to rallies with like-minded retirees.

Then their mortality began to weigh on me a little. When Dad turned 70, I realized for the first time that they were getting old. Dad developed COPD and his last five years were much more sedate than before. Mom had a heart attack once that they didn't tell me about for a couple of months because they didn't want me to worry. They had both had colonoscopies as a standard course of examina-tion, and it was discovered that Mom had colon cancer. I flew out to be there with them while Mom had surgery in January of 1998. Dad was really scared. He and I thought we were going to lose her. I gained a new perspective on their relationship, and how it had changed from when I was a teen. They had become an affectionate, aging couple who had grown to accept each other and enjoy the life they shared. I was really scared for both of them. Throughout my life, Mom having surgery was a common occurrence. This turned out to be *Mom's Last Surgery*.

MOM'S LAST SURGERY

January
Colon surgery scheduled
Accommodating busy daughter,
I insisted
I be there.
Arrived Phoenix night before
Daddy befuddled
Scared for her
For himself.
"Thank God
You're here."

Mom congested
Lied to doctor
Unwilling to postpone.
Smell of fear
Permeated the air
She slept in her recliner
Unable to breathe
Lying down.
Scream awakened
I flew from my room
Tackling lamp and table
Gashing my shin.
Found Mom
Face down
Blanket tangled
Recliner foot-rest,
Fat lip bleeding.

Dad and I
Set her right
Tomorrow's outlook
Gloomier, grimmer.
Back in bed
Shin throbbing,
Sobbing for them
For me.
Thank God
I was there.

Dad
Eighty in a month
Never had I seen him
So full of fear.
Surgery successful
Life after surgery
Tentative.
Dad sat bedside
Helpless.
Family hospital advocate essential
She could still die.
I knew
I was her only hope.
Thank God
I was there.

Stomach tube
Oxygen
IV drip
Catheter
Leg circulation cuffs.
She could not
Clear her throat, lungs
Pneumonia imminent.
My throat became raw
Demonstrating.

Lunches, dinners
Hospital café with Dad
Bad food, but
No worse than
Country Kitchen Senior Buffet.
Good talks
Daddy and I
In my memory, first time
Just us two, no Mom
Butting in, taking over.
A time I treasure.
Storytelling Dad's forte
His memory full,
Past came alive.

He revealed
Secret wallet pocket
Cash stash
Hidden from Mom.
"You never know
When you'll need it."
He told me
He loved Mom, feared
She might die.
Reassuringly
She's tough, I told him
Yeah,
A tough old bird.

Tougher than he
It turned out.

M om recovered, and in April, four months later, it was Dad's turn. He had a large polyp that could only be removed by surgery. I went back to Phoenix for a repeat performance. Dad was stronger than Mom, so I figured all would be well. He came out of the surgery in good shape and seemed so much better than Mom did, that we were relieved and relaxed. Dad was an expert at hocking and spitting, so I had no worries about his lungs filling with fluid. On the second night after surgery, Mom and I put the rails up and left around 9 pm. He had been given a shot of pain medication and was drifting off as we pulled up his blankets. After we got home and were ready for bed, having had the obligatory cup of hot milk, Mom's nightly ritual, we got a call that Dad had fallen and was in intensive care. We changed back out of our pajamas and raced back to the hospital to find Dad in a coma, on a ventilator, with no brain activity.

Mom was devastated and weak. I was probably in some state of shock. I kept thinking that he was fine two hours ago when we left him, what the hell had happened? We stayed for awhile then I drove Mom back home to get some sleep. We had talked to the neurologist on call, and Dad's prognosis was not good. In the morning, I called for backup. I wanted to have Phil, Dennis, Darin and my sister, Diane come and join me in Phoenix. I thought that since he wasn't dead yet, they could at least say their goodbyes, and I felt I could not do this by myself. The neurologist spoke with all of us and showed us an EEG that indicated Daddy was brain dead. He strongly suggested we take Dad off the ventilator since there was nothing else that could be done. We reluctantly agreed. The neurologist said that Dad would probably die within an hour or so, and the hospital personnel told us to say our last goodbyes and then they'd call us when he actually died. Always the rebel, I said, "No way! We're not going to leave him here to die alone!" So, we took him off life support and for hours, watched him die. It was not pretty. *Daddy's Demise, Parts I-IV: Pre-Op, Toenails, Beginning of the End* and *Bedside Vigil* tell of his last days and hours.

DADDY'S DEMISE
PART I — PRE-OP

Surgical removal necessary
Colonoscopy sighted polyp
Too large.
Phoenix
Repeat performance
Hospital routine
Changing places
Mom, Dad.

Dad pre-op,
Donned surgery blues
Elastic hairnet bonnet
Clown like
Reveals mother
Within her son.

Belongings
Handed loved ones
Shoes pants underwear
All visible
Clear drawstring
Plastic bag,
Crime scene evidence
Exhibit A.

Dad's toenails
Snagged blue booties.
Sitting waiting
Foot in lap
I casually
Trimmed toenails
First one foot
Then the other.
Memories
Daddy clipping my nails,
Welled up inside me
Filled my eyes.

Big man,
Often too big, looked
Small, old, afraid.
Age shrinks the body
Fear shrinks the soul.

His name called
Nurse waiting
Clipboard in hand.
Panic twinge
Gripped my heart
Mom visibly shaken
One last hug.
Split gown wafted
Double doors closed
Behind him
Leaving only prayer.

We waited Mom and I
Where Dad and I sat
Four months before.
Mom barely recovered from
Her own ordeal.

These people, my parents
I loved
Feared
Ran from
Longed for
Reduced to this.
Nature's cruel lesson
Knowing when to leave.

PART II —
TOENAILS

Daddy survived surgery
Recovery progressed
Relief sighs breathed
Out of the woods.

Blanket too short
Dad's feet stuck out
Left foot
Toenails untrimmed
Right foot trimmed
Twice?
Outward calm
Could not disguise
My inner fear.
Betrayed by
Toenails.

PART III —
BEGINNING OF THE END

Hospital room boredom
Laptop solitaire playing
Daddy's last request
Can we talk a while?
Heartfelt conversation
Always kept at bay.

Exhausted,
Daddy drugged,
Side rails raised,
Tubes inserted
Every orifice
Loved ones head home.

Nightly
Hot milk ritual over
Teeth brushed
Horizontal heaven welcomed.

Ringing phone
Pierced bedtime silence
Changed lives
Forever.

Conflicting stories
Tell tale.
Despite restraints
Daddy got up
Fell down
Code Blue.
Sirens lured
Aged Odysseus
Peaceful life beyond, then
Left him for dead
Gasping
On the shore.

Slumber deprived
Head spinning
Hysterical,
Family returned
Health care crime scene.
Nearly naked
Head gashed
Doctors, techs
ICU bedside
Working Daddy over
Prognosis grim.

PART IV —

BEDSIDE VIGIL

Unable
Face doom, death alone,
Reinforcements called in
Husband, sons, sister
Dad wasn't dead,
Yet.

Seated round sterile table
Neurologist broke news
EEG, scientific facts
Sealed Daddy's fate.
Brain dead, no hope
End life support
Only rational decision.

Hospital staff expected
Last goodbyes,
Leave Dad
Die
In capable hands.
Not so fast
Dad doesn't die alone
ICU family vigil
Encircled Dad's bed.

Nurse administered morphine
Comfort dose
Again
And again.
Common practice
Uncomfortable
Unsettling
Agonizing hours
Dragged on.
Silently shrinking Mom
In shock, growing
Weaker
Sadder.

One by one whispering
Personal goodbye messages
Me forgiving
Asking forgiveness.
Finally
Fatal last breath
Flat-line.
Tears
Sadness
Relief
Intense relief.
Grandson,
Felt Dad's humiliation
Removed
Black rubber tongue restrictor.
Hospital rules
Stripped death's dignity.

Medical examiner
Kept body
Autopsy ordered
Cause of death unclear.
Clinical analysis
One body part
At a time.
Life's final insult.

O f course, death is just the beginning for those who did not die. Many decisions had to be made: what to do with his remains, whether to have a service, and what to do about Mother. We also had our lives waiting for us at home. Mom and Dad had jointly decided to be cremated since they thought the entire funeral system was a rip-off. Mom decided that she did not want a service since most of their friends were either already dead or were other motor coach traveling retirees living out of state. *Next of Kin* and *Funeral Home* take Dad's soulless body and give him back to us in a cardboard canister. His death and the events that followed have had a profound affect on my life and the lives of my family. I expressed my feelings about death in *Grim Reaper.*

NEXT OF KIN

Autopsy in progress,
Brain on ice,
Medical examiner
Released Dad's body.
Loved one needed,
Proper Identification
Precedes
Return to dust.

So peaceful he looked
I ran my fingers through his
White wavy hair
Hugged his neck
One last time
Final
Father daughter parting.
Familiar
Physical connection, yet
Dad's spirit
Long gone.
At rest
Or
In line for new life.
We may meet again.

FUNERAL HOME

Chapel of the Chimes
Funeral home director
Young Brandon
Welcomed bereaved family.
Formal conference setting
Daddy's knights
Around table,
Wife, daughters
Son-in-law, grandsons.

Brandon spoke
Mother gasped.
"Ghoulish"
She leaned, whispered.
Brandon's braces,
Elastic bands
Created Addams Family
Atmosphere.

Legal questions answered
Casket room awaited.
But, Dad's being
Cremated.
No matter.
"You may choose
Make his final
Emblazing
Elegant."
Brandon
Bets his business
On guilt.

"Walk This Way"
Beckoned Brandon.
Always a wit,
Mother,
Widow for a day
Winked at us
Did ghoul-walk
Dragging one leg.
Suddenly giddy
Dying of suppressed
Laughter
Ghoul-walking crowd
Followed Mom.

Caskets
Ranging in thousands
Rejected.
"We'll take that one."
Practical
Cardboard box chosen.
This crowd's guilt
Self-inflicted,
Not phased by
Undertaker's attempts.
Ming ash urn

Also pooh-poohed.
Temporary
Cardboard container favored.

We had already
Pulled the plug.
This part was
Easy.

GRIM REAPER

Death.
Grim Reaper
Mysterious worker.
Prior to personal experience
My sorrow
Directed at departed
They'll never do this
Never see that.
My naïveté
Innocence,
Almost laughable.

Always,
All about us
Our connection
With the dead,
What we will miss,
What we will never do
With them
Again.
We grieve for ourselves.
The dead
Dearly departed,
Gone.
Dead and gone.

Living
Left standing
Face to face with death
Our death.

M om was weak and seemed to be teetering between wishing
she could just walk off the planet with Dad and be done with
it, and knowing she had to live on. She couldn't stay in
Phoenix alone, grieving, barely recovered from surgery, so Phil and
I brought her home to New Jersey to live with us. She didn't want
to go and leave Phoenix, her home for 40 years. It was her sense of
place, of their life together, and like most surviving spouses, she did-
n't know anywhere else. I really didn't want to bring her home with
me either. Phil and I had been married less than two years. But, she
was too weak to stay by herself. She knew it and I knew it. It was
the only choice. We packed her bags, a few files and flew her to her
new home. *Herself* speaks of my fear and resentment.

HERSELF

Flying
Arizona to New Jersey
Mother's transplanting
Her house to mine.
Paralyzing thoughts
Future with Mom.
Phil did not know her,
I knew her
Too well.

Eighteen months
Newly married
We knew
There was no other way.
Kind, loving, willing
Was I
Hateful, resentful, dreading
Was I.
Guilty, selfish
Was I.
After all this time
Here I am
Saddled with Mom.

I barely knew
My father,
She never allowed it.
Now he's dead
And I'm stuck
With her.
No time to mourn him,
No service,
She couldn't bear it.
It was always
About her.

After Mom confessed her sin, she had settled into a comfortable
routine with us in New Jersey. We knew that what was left
behind in Phoenix had to be dealt with sooner or later, so in
June, two months after Dad died, Mom, Darin and I returned to
Phoenix. We needed to sort out her belongings, sell the house and
the motor coach, and leave Phoenix for good. Mom wanted to have
a garage sale. She had a friend in Mesa, a garage sale aficionado who
had agreed to come and help with it. I conceded although I would

rather have given her any amount of money to skip the sale and paid someone to haul it all away instead.

Our strong intentions must have preceded us, because we listed and sold the house, found a buyer for the motor coach, and had the garage sale all within a week. We shipped some things to Diane in California, gave some stuff away, and sold everything else, except the car and Mom's blue recliner. *Garage Sale* and *Leaving Arizona* is the record of our adventure. Mom and I flew back to New Jersey afterward and Darin drove Mom's red Saturn.

GARAGE SALE

Three generations
Return
Scene of the crime.
Garage sale
Major event,
Main attraction.

June in Phoenix
106 degrees in the shade
Garage sale
No way out.
Gladly given Mom
Any amount,
Donated everything.
But no,
The sale must go on.

Mom's friends arrived
Kindly offering help
Lugging, pricing.
Some items
Never made sale tables
Compressor
Flatware set
Dad's clothes
Underwear out of hamper
Into grocery bags,
Into friend's van.

Everything neatly displayed on
Carport tables
Sheet-covered
Like rows of corpses.
Use and Care booklets available
All appliances large and small
Diligently filed
Waiting
For this day.

Early AM door bell
Startled all.
Professional shoppers
Anxious cherry pickers.
Five-thirty too early
Sent away 'til seven.
Long hot day loomed ahead
Morning coffee consumed
Awaiting scavenger armies.

Mother and son
Each other's only sanity,
Often eye connected,
"What are we doing
Here?"
His presence a blessing
Sharing wakeful nightmare.

Indignant assessment
Toothless, dirty, scraggly,
Grubbing vultures
Profiting, capitalizing
Another's pain, loss.
Realizing
We invited them
Sent us reeling,
Vacillating between
Heatstroke induced
Light-headed laughter,
And tears.

Sadness
Heartbreaking anguish
My parents' entire life
Spread before me.
Watching worldly goods
Rummaged through,
Touched by unwashed hands.
Strangers judging
Lifelong purchase decisions
Taken as treasures
Rejected as garbage.
Painful to me,
Closure for her.

LEAVING ARIZONA

Dad dead two months
Cleanup crew returned
Valley of the Sun
Our mission,
Disposal.
Everything must go.
House
Motor coach
Furniture
Tupperware
All worldly goods
Barring
Favorite blue recliner.

After robbing the bank of
Safe deposit riches
Surviving garage sale
No place left to sit
Before flight
Her new home
My home.

Overwhelming mixed emotions
Avoid eye contact
At all costs
Disney movie perfect alternative
Soft seats
No conversation required.

Walking through the mall
I saw her anew.
Old, frail woman
Lost, disoriented
Pocketbook clutched closely
Only thing left.

Sitting too close
Watching previews,
I remembered
She hated
Going to movies.

We saw Mulan
Brave woman warrior.
Mom stared blankly
She didn't know
The movie
Was about her.
Woman
In a man's job
Woman
Being brave
In the face of
Adversity
Fear.

As I looked at her
My throat swelled
My chest heaved.
Everything gone
Daddy,
Her 55 year companion,
Her home
Her belongings.
Everything familiar
Surrendered,
Unknown city
Strange surroundings
Her new life.

I sobbed
In the darkness
While Mulan
Won her battle.

The transition was difficult for all of us. Phil and I went to work every day leaving Mom home alone. Our house is very isolated, located in a quiet rural neighborhood. It took a few more months for Mom to get comfortable with her new life and for us to adjust. Having Mom with me every day was a unique and strange experience. It made me think deeply about my life, who I am, and how heredity and family all fit together. I have always been somewhat interested in genetics, in what makes us who we are. Our first introduction to genetics occurs when we're quite small, and people say "Oh, she looks just like her mother or father or grandparent." I always thought that the genetic part had most to do with physical attributes and hereditary diseases, but not so much other traits, such as facial expressions, behavioral patterns, speech patterns, and personality. Those I figured were learned or due to astrology or other forces of nature.

There's a fine line between nurture and nature, and through my first hand experience with Mom, I'm becoming increasingly convinced that genetics may account for more of who we are at our core and the learned behaviors are what we try to replace those natural tendencies with. Since so much of our learning takes place at such an early age the lines get blurred, and things that are innate could be assumed to be learned. As little children, all we want to do is emulate, mimic and essentially be just like our parents. Our minds log and categorize every detail of every situation with them. And then we spend a lifetime trying to change these conditioned responses. At least that's how it has been with me.

I was a rather rebellious young woman. During my teens, whether it was discipline, attitude, religion, values, or just the living of life in general, I often swore that I would not treat my children the way my parents treated me. I would not act the way they acted or *be* the way they were, when I grew up. I especially didn't want to be like my mother. I hated being told I looked like her, or resembled her in any way. All I wanted to do was get away from my parents and be free to be myself, whoever that was.

It was when I had children that it started. I recall scolding Dennis, "You're acting just like a two-year-old." It was a phrase Mom used throughout my teens. Dennis *was* two though, and I was becoming my mother. At times my mouth would open, and it was Mom speaking not me. I had to double my efforts and be ever mindful of this unwanted person lurking just below the surface.

Phil met Marian and Scob before we were married. He said, "You and your mom are like twins!" Phil kept looking from me, to Mom, to me again, and was astonished at the similarities: our voices, our laughs, our faces, our expressions and gestures. He couldn't get over it. My first reaction was denial and horror. That could have been the end of a beautiful relationship. I figured either he'd dump me because I was like Mom, or I'd dump him because he thought so. Instead, for the first time, I understood that being like Mom was not a total negative. He really enjoyed her. Phil said she was friendly, funny, quick witted, mouthy, and cynical. "Many of the things I love about you," he told me.

Years ago, if you had asked me what I would do when one of my parents died, I would have said I didn't know, but I never would have thought I would have my mother live with me. Then, as fate twisted and Mom was living with us, I began to look at her in a different light, more as a person, rather than as some kind of extension of me. I began to allow myself to see the parallels between us, and appreciate the parts of her that I had incorporated, the gifts she had given me. I realized Mom had been my mentor without my knowing it, working most of her life in traditionally men's jobs. She had a great work ethic, and balanced her career and family. She was determined, driven, perceptive, intuitive, and a detective. The list goes on.

I had no idea what to expect, living with Mother. I hadn't spent more than one week a year with her for the last 25 years. I thought it would seem like having a stranger in the house, but I was wrong. It was more like looking into a mirror, an outward and inward mirror. This is where the line between genetics and learned behavior gets very blurry for me. The thing is, I knew her thoughts. Not all of them, of course, but in many situations, I felt I could look at her and know what she was thinking and feeling. I realized I was being presented with the thoughts and feelings that I worked so hard to change in myself. Now, here they were, right in front of me again. The difference was that they were no longer in my head or in my guts, but rather in hers. Also, I finally had the courage to tell her what I saw and sensed in a loving way. I was no longer hateful or resentful for having felt or thought the way she did, for being like her. Instead, I am thankful for having been given the chance to once more learn and grow from this woman I chose as my mother.

In October, six months after Dad died, we decided to have a ceremony, a small family service to acknowledge Dad's death. Mom finally felt up to it. Darin suggested that we plant a tree in his honor in the yard. We did, and mixed his ashes in with the soil. It was a beautiful day and Diane and her family came from California to join us. I wrote *Ashes to Ashes* to commemorate the ceremony.

ASHES TO ASHES

Stowed beneath
Airplane seat
Green duffel concealed
Cardboard carton
Containing Dad.
Ashes
Bone fragments
Teeth.
190 pounds flesh
10 pounds dust.

Silently
Dad sat
Six months
Hall closet.

Back yard burial
Plant a tree
In memoriam
Dad's entire extended family
In attendance.

Freshly turned soil
Smelled of life
Sobbing
Kneeling
I poured Dad's ashes
Into the hole
His grandsons dug.
Fertilizer now
Sapling, pink dogwood.

Black Hawk Speaks
Eulogy to Dad.
At Mom's request,
Son-in-law sang
Amazing Grace.
Hands joined
Will the Circle Be Unbroken
Chanted.
Sweet simple sacred service.
Fitting for the
Dad
I wish I had known better.

The ceremony was good for Mom, brought closure and a release. That coupled with her freedom from her great secret, my brother, gave her a new lease on life. She pulled herself together, acclimating to her new home and environs. She seemed happy. She got her NJ driver's license, re-registered her car, bought insurance, and began driving in this new town. She walked on the treadmill almost everyday. She became our administrative assistant, handling the mail and bills and learned Quicken, the automated personal finance software. The only thing she asked for every day was a hug before going to bed. Dad was a good hugger. She spent a lot of time alone, but was motivated to join women's and senior clubs. She made friends easily and had a wonderful and fulfilling last life chapter. She had lunch plans every Wednesday, played Canasta every Thursday, and attended free senior discussions and speaker sessions offered by the local hospital. Mom hadn't had a birthday party since she was five, so in October, we planned her 80th birthday party which was a very special day filled with family, new friends, joy and happiness. Pictures of her glowing with trees dressed in their most colorful foliage behind her tell the story better than I can.

After her birthday, Mom got pneumonia twice and ended up in the hospital in January. She was there for two weeks and when she was ready to leave, she couldn't walk. I did not understand. I thought that with a little work she could get her function back. I was wrong. I wrote *Denial*.

DENIAL

You don't understand
Two weeks ago
Mom was driving
Met her friends
Played canasta
Laughed.

Two weeks in here
You've turned her into
An invalid!
She can't walk
She can't fend
For herself.

What have you done?
You don't understand.

I did not understand.

M om spent a couple of months at home with a health aide 10-12 hours a day. She suggested that she move to an assisted living facility, while she'd still be accepted as semi-independent. She thought it would be better to have people her own age around rather than being home alone with the health aide. So, we began searching for a place that would suit her. We found a great place with caring staff and many residents in similar shape as Mom. We moved her to Fellowship Village in early March. I visited every day, hating to see her there. She was only there for two months. If we knew she would not survive longer than that, we would have kept her home, but how could any of us, including Mom, have predicted the future? *Last Days* chronicles her time there. Our last conversation was on a Friday, described in *I'm Dying*.

LAST DAYS

There
Less than two months
Assisted Living
Fellowship Village
Her choice
I think.

Antibiotics again
Bronchitis.
Dehydrated,
Mom never liked
The taste
Of water.

After work
Go Sit Chat.
Watery oatmeal
Dry chicken
Mean aides
Accidents
Gossip
Comings and goings
Of strangers.
Jeopardy
The Wheel
Nightly fare.

I longed for
Real conversation.
I dreamed
Joyful
Lighthearted visits
Laughter,
Sense of humor, wit
Her best traits.

I imagined
Journaling her story
Only one left to tell it
Our ancestors
Past secrets
Prisons
Psychological thriller.

Instead
Visits drifted
Meaningless
Unfocused.
Disintegrated
Exhausted
No patience.

Bedtime ritual
Elastic stockings
Pajamas
Good night hug
Requisite since Daddy died,
A really good hugger he.

I'M DYING

Losing function
Weakness
I didn't understand
High speed chase
Racing against time
Toward death.

Do you think I'm dying?
I don't know.
Do you?

Friday night
Our last conversation
Face to face
How could I
Have known?

That night
I could have said
Heartfelt things
Held her
Loved her
Tenderly.

That night
Particularly weak
Unable
Stand up unaided
Take even
One step.

That night
Particularly afraid
Getting in bed
Falling out of bed.

I struggled
Helping her
Rag doll limp
Commode
Diaper
Pajamas.

So afraid
Shouting out for help
For an aide
Didn't she see
I was there
Her daughter?
Didn't she know
I was capable
Of helping her?

It's ok
It's ok.
I'm here.
You're not
Going
  To
    Fall.

Leaning over
Holding her
Crying
It's going to be
Ok
I love you
Mommy.

Painful
See her like that
Difficult
Leave her like that
Impossible
Stay
One
More
Minute.

I fled through slow
Wheelchair accessible automatic doors.
Parking lot safe
Head on the steering wheel
Sobbing
For her
For me.

Do you think
I'm dying?
Yes, Mom
On Wednesday.

T he following Sunday, Mother's Day, 2000, she went to the hospital for the last time. She had pneumonia again and was so dehydrated she could not swallow. Again I called Diane to come. This time at least, Mom was conscious, but just barely. We were in and out of the hospital all day long for three days. We did not, as some families do, set up a bed and vigil there around the clock. It did not occur to me to do that, or to Diane. We were just 10 minutes away. Tuesday evening, she was talking of falling down a hole and asking for help. She joked a little with Phil, something she loved doing. We left her for the night and returned home. I called the hospital early the next morning to see how she fared over night and they said she was doing fine, so I went to work. Diane was going to the hospital after breakfast. By 9 am, I received a call from the hospital that she had died.

When I walked into her room, the oxygen mask had been removed but her head was leaning back and her mouth was gaping open as if she were gasping for breath. Her thin skeleton was already ghostlike. That vision of her there in that bed with no one holding her hand, no one encircling her bed as we had with Dad, and dying alone, haunted me. On the fourth anniversary of her death, May 17, 2004, I wrote *Ghost Talk*, which helped quiet the unnecessary guilt.

GHOST TALK

Labyrinth walking
Your ashes
Under my feet
Conversation easy
Knowing you're listening.

So many years we spent
Apart
Your absence
Not unusual.
Blessed were we
After Dad's death
Your last two years
We lived together.

Your thoughts
Spoke loudly
I knew you so well
Despite your secrets.
A mirror you were
Reflecting
Who I am
Who I strove
Not to be.

I pray, God's grace
Allows me
Keep the best of you,
Your worst
With your bones
Up in smoke.
Path stones quiver
Acknowledgement.

I forgive you
Your absence
Times I needed you most.
Forgive me
For letting you
Die
Alone.

M om was a very strong woman, and after Dad died, she was
determined to get back in the game of life. She did not go
down without a fight. After her death, when I looked back
at her, the drama and tragedy of both Mom and Dad's death behind
me, I saw a beautiful and courageous woman. My resentments have
melted and I can honestly say I am honored to be her daughter. I
hope I am like her. I wrote *My Mother, My Self* after contemplating
the question of who my mentor was.

MY MOTHER, MY SELF

Who is the woman who taught you
How to be?
They ask.
They want to be like her, too.
Maybe they want to be
Like me.
She was many women,
She was quite a woman,
This woman, my mom.

Courageous and independent
A Depression daughter,
Working and helping her family
Even though her father
"Didn't need her help."
She was Rosie the Riveter
Helping her country
Her first man's job
First of many.

Wife and mother
Not without loss
Not without suffering
One boy surrendered
One boy lost before birth
Blue Baby Freddie
Lived only 5 days.
Two girls survived to tell
Her tale.

She became a vagabond
For the sake of her child
First Florida
Next Arizona
Friends and familiarity
Left behind.

She joined the workforce
For good this time
At the bottom
Where women belonged
But not for long.

She was smart
She was funny
She was on the move
Gloria had nothing on her
She was a libber
Before it was in fashion.

I never knew I had
Paid such close attention.
Her story became my story
How can that be?
I tried
To be like anyone
But her.
It did not work.

I never lost a child
As she did.
I grew up with
Women's Lib, but
I was not a pioneer
As she was.
I knew
I could do anything
Because she went before me
Taught me
Paved my way.

I hope I
Have trail blazed for others
Cleared their path
Eased their burdens.
It's the least
I could do
In her name.

CHAPTER SEVEN

Dig Deeper,
Think the Unthinkable

T he mind is so tricky, at least mine is. I had not gone to a doctor for a knee diagnosis because I knew that I would be told I had minor meniscus tears or a breakdown of cartilage or something, and that I should have some kind of laser surgery to repair it. I had seen this so often with friends and co-workers. Once the knee was repaired, the pain moved to their shoulder or back and they returned to the surgeon for rotator cuff or back procedures. I just didn't want to buy into it. I knew my knee pain was mine and mine alone, not the result of accident or injury. I didn't want my head to be further screwed up with a physical diagnosis. But, that little grain of doubt kept me teetering, and kept me in pain, willingly falling back on the germ of a thought that the problem could be physical and then I wouldn't have to dig any further. Finally, I made an appointment to go see Dr. Sarno to get a confirmation that I had TMS, this physical manifestation that causes pain, or I didn't.

Originally, Sarno had focused on this physiological alteration of muscles and tendons, but has since broadened his theory to encompass what he terms as TMS equivalents, which include gastrointestinal, circulatory, skin, immune system, genitourinary, and cardiac disorders. He has also included fibromyalgia and chronic fatigue syndrome as equivalents, and sees unconscious emotions as playing a role in the causation of autoimmune disorders like rheumatoid

arthritis as well as cancer. His new book, *The Divided Mind,* reiter-
ates the TMS syndrome, calling it the epidemic of mindbody disorders.

On physical examination, Sarno confirmed that I was suffering
from TMS. In our conversation, as I was giving him a bit of my history, he realized that I had had bouts of TMS and its equivalents,
going back to my original diagnosis of Irritable Bowel Syndrome
half my life ago. I knew IBS was stress induced but I also often
thought IBS could be genetic since Mom had so much colon relat-
ed trouble. When my hips started killing me at night sometime
before my knee began to hurt, I figured it was also genetic since my
dad had what he called, "bad hips." Sarno assured me these were all
manifestations of the same thing. He explained how the brain will
pull switches and substitutions when it is no longer effective causing
pain in a certain area. He arranged for me to come back for his next
lecture. I went home that night relieved that nothing physical was
wrong and also feeling weighed down with the knowledge that only
I could heal my knee. I wrote *Sacred Vessel.*

S ACRED V ESSEL

Truth
Truth
Wicked, wonderful
Truth!
Blessing and
Curse.

Self
Bearer, carrier, cause
All misery, sickness
Physical
Mental.

Self
Keeper of the cure
Held deep within,
Private
Pandora's Box.

Don't let them out
They'll bring
Plague, pestilence.
Keep them in, hidden
They'll only
Kill you.
Quickly, slowly
As you wish.

Diagnosis confirmed
No physical injury
Pain
Unconsciously manifested.

Frantic search
Physical remedy
Spiritual problem
Proves elusive.
Seek rather
Spiritual cure
Physical problem.
Readily available
To the seeker
Waiting patiently
Below the mind's surface.

Patient not doctor
Sole provider
Soul medicine
Prescriber.

Inner pain
Hideous, insidious
Deeply imbedded
Every cell
All tissue.

Surgeries
Recoveries
Rehabilitations
Easy by comparison
Preferred by most.

Redecision
Renewal
Rejuvenation
Possible only
From the inside
Out.

Aghhhhhhh,
Excruciating knowledge
Joy, happiness, health
I alone hold the key
I alone can choose.
Aye,
There's the rub.

O nce diagnosed and armed with my confirmed knowledge having attended Dr. Sarno's lecture, I understood for certain that the cure for my knee was within me. Dr. Sarno advised me, as he does most of his patients, that there were no restrictions on my activity. Even if I was experiencing pain, he explained I was not injuring myself more by moving or exercising the painful area. As soon as I felt comfortable resuming my normal routines, I was to do so, and so I did, in pain or not. Some days the pain eased. Some days it would come raging back. Some days I would basically hobble along, barely putting weight on my left leg. I tried not to feel defeated. After all this writing, my knee still was not right. It was difficult not to give in to defeat and search for that physical cure. When I looked again at my list of rage topics, I knew I had more work to do.

Two issues kept coming to the front of my mind, the affect my brother had on me through my parents and my career. I had worked since I was a teen, and being a single mother I had to work to live, so my career had become a huge part of my life. Some changes that occurred in my last couple of years of working definitely had to be dealt with. But, family first.

Even saying the word brother makes me pause, since this is a man I have never met or even spoken to, and whom until six years ago, did not exist in my world. Melding my parents' knowing into the mix in my mind of life with Mom and Dad, it came out sideways. I thought of my dad. I never had the chance to talk to him about my brother, and according to Mom, they never discussed it after the fact. My heart bleeds for him and the angst he must have held inside with the silence. I also reexamined my relationship with Dad looking through the "brother filter." I tried to imagine his actions as emanating from a different emotional or motive base. *Scob* and *Daddy's Girl* resulted.

SCOB

Your pain source
Revealed
Posthumously
Finally
I understand.

Baby boy lost
Cast away
Lies
Procrastination
Fear.
Had you any idea
It would come to this?
Had you any idea
Mom's resentment would last
For life?

Couples regularly survive
Heartache
Loss
Pain
Love conquers all
Not so.
No compassion
No spoken forgiveness
Not for you.

DADDY'S GIRL

Having given away
His first-born son
Lost his second
Miscarriage,
Daddy's
Disappointment
My female gender
Etched on my psyche
Since birth.

Childhood lessons,
Methods, tactics
Garner notice
Acceptance
Love.
Try harder
Be good
Be the best
Please.
Be whatever they want
Me to be.

Don't be naughty
Like my sister
Suffer Mother's wrath.
Be goody-two-shoes
A-student
Mother's confidant
Daddy's son.

Fondest memories
With Dad
Lionel train
Rifle practice
Fishing.
Teenage sharp shooter
Ace angler.

Tomboy,
Always siding
Against my own kind,
Needed boys to
Like me
Trust me.
Couldn't bear
Boyish taunts
Directed at
Giggly, silly
Sissy girls.

So uncomfortable in
My skin
Shedding impossible
Chose
Chameleon survival strategy,
Be best son
Dad could have
Asked for.

I kept thinking of Sarno's suggestion to "think the unthinkable," and allowed myself to think like a spoiled child or a selfish adult brat. I'm not at all sure where the next two poems, *Cry for Love*, and *Thoroughly Modern Mother*. came from, except vaguely remembered conversations with Mom, telling stories of my infancy and babyhood. Perhaps there are memories stashed at the unconscious and cellular level from infancy. Some of it is purely my imaginings of a time past.

CRY FOR LOVE

Momma,
Pick me up
Hold me.
Please
Hold me close.
I don't need anything
But you.

Do you think
You don't deserve me
After giving
My brother away?
Are you
Punishing yourself
By punishing me?
Brother's gone
But I'm here.

I'm not hungry
I'm not wet
I'm crying
For you.
Can't your heart
Hear me?

You marvel
I drink from
Propped bottle
Hold my own
All by myself.
Praised from infancy
Self-sufficiency
Intellect
Aloneness.
Momma
Won't you hold me
While you feed me
Another's milk?
I'm alone
I'm lonely
In my crib.

Where's Daddy?
Can't he hold me?
Have you convinced him
He too
Doesn't deserve me?
Is your resentment
Guilt
So strong?

Daddy's fault
Brother's gone.
Brother's gone,
But I'm here.

You are good enough
You are deserving
You are perfect
For me.
Momma, please
Love yourself
So I can learn
To love
Me.

THOROUGHLY MODERN MOTHER

Let her cry.
"Spare the rod
Spoil the child."
Momma
Don't believe
Spock's lie.
Listen
Hear your heart
Don't let some expert
Cheat you.
Soothing your child
Mother's greatest joy
Strongest bond
Lifetime scars.

Carnation
"Better for your baby."
Momma,
Don't believe
Big business' lie
Nothing's better than
God's
Natural nourishment.
I need you
Not chemicals
And cows.

I thought about all the hateful feelings and resentment I ever felt toward my parents and just let it spew forth without judgment or throttle. *Child Within* and *Narcissistic Injury* are examples of my deeper digging into my mind's recesses in that "unthinkable" mode. I feel somewhat embarrassed and petty for writing them, but they needed to be written.

CHILD WITHIN: UNCONSCIOUS REPRESSED RAGE RANTING

MOM

You wielded guilt
A knight's sword
Jabbing, slicing major arteries.
Always complaining
About Dad, Diane
I could never
Just be myself
I knew you'd hate me too.
Carrying your heavy baggage
I buckled under its weight.

You didn't stand up for me
You let Dad beat me
Black and blue
With his belt,
You watched
Said nothing
Did nothing.
My sister sat
Watched, sobbed, wailed,
"Just cry, he'll stop!"
I wouldn't cry,
Give him the satisfaction
That he hurt me.

Because of you
I had no relationship
With Dad.
You were jealous
You were always there
Butting in.
Dad could never even
Finish a sentence.
You emasculated him,
Complained
He treated you so poorly.

You blamed Diane and me
For your lot in life,
Told us you wished we had
Never been born.
You were gutless
You could have left
Instead you stayed
Tortured us all.

DAD

You were pathetic.
You let Mom
Walk all over you.
You never stood up for yourself
Never said, Enough!
It wasn't all your fault
But you let Mom
Wallow in her resentment toward you
Make all our lives miserable.

How could you beat me
Like that?
Did you forget
Think I was Mom?
Source of the anger
You took out on me.

In the end, Dad
You couldn't even order
What you wanted to eat
At a restaurant.
So worn out by years of
Capitulation
Resignation
"I'll have what she's having,"
Misery.

MOM & DAD

Neither of you
Ever came clean
About James Thomas.
You lived a lie
Your entire lives
Never discussed
Your son.
You let your misery
Eat you alive
Passed the parasite on to us.

Then, one day
The curse was broken
Sleeping Beauty and Rip Van Winkle
You woke to a silent peace
You seemed to forget.
Holding hands when walking,
No more fighting,
Placid acceptance
Or love?

I loved you both
Wanted your love
In return.
I know in my heart
You did love me
Very much
The only way you could.

On your death beds
I asked your forgiveness
For all my wrongs,
Forgave you yours.

When I speak to you now
Address your ghosts
It is from love
Shared ancestry
Gratitude
For giving me life.

NARCISSISTIC INJURY

Lifetime spent
Being perfect
Overachiever
Perfectionist
Progressive workaholic
Super Mom.
I can do that attitude
Served me well.

Lost in my perception of who
I thought you wanted
Me to be
There was no me
To be.

Occasionally
Unbearable pressure
Blew gaskets,
Worn-thin chains broke
I became worse
Than you or I could imagine.
But, that wasn't
Really me
Either
Just attempts at
Removing the mask.

Unconscious
Childhood foundation
Paved adulthood path.

I had to be
Better than the rest
So no one would ever know
I was not good enough.
I had to make
Men love me
So no one would ever know
I was not lovable.
I had to excel
In men's jobs
So no one would ever know
I was the wrong gender.

Half century later
I have learned
Be myself
Love myself
Please myself
Experience joy.
My true nature,
Goodness, compassion.
Today, I can
Be good, do good
For my sake.

I know now
You loved me
Never meant to hurt me
I know now
You did the best
You could.
It is
Enough.

I still think my childhood was reasonably common. Not common perhaps in the details, but in the ordinariness of surviving in a day-to-day existence that doesn't leave much room for intro-spection. When couples have issues between them and when they are also struggling to make a living, a life for themselves and their children, there isn't much time or desire to dig through the past or address the present. My folks did what was in front of them as well as they could, avoiding pain as much as possible. I cannot and do not judge them, regardless of some of my ranting. I know they were proud of me and I of them. Writing about them in this way has allowed me to let go of any ill-will and see them and love them for who they were, with all their blemishes and weaknesses, as I hope my children will do for me. I respected and was touched by their sweet togetherness in the winter of their lives. They needed each other more than they needed freedom from the wounds of the past.

CHAPTER EIGHT

Working Woman

M y career, my life's work from my first job in a sewing shop at age thirteen to Managing Director at a major Wall Street stock brokerage firm has always been a source of great joy and pride to me as well as a source of income. I always worked hard and tried to work smart. The blood, sweat and tears I poured into my work were returned to me in many ways, monetary reward being just one of them. I worked as a seamstress and a waitress. I was a keypunch operator, a programmer, systems analyst and designer. I managed teams, groups, departments and divisions. It was all good. As I progressed through my career, I became more myself, more confident, and more understanding. Two things brought me the most joy, seeing the results of a job well done, and people. Working with and watching people learn, develop, grow and change made long hours and painful work situations worthwhile.

I had laid a foundation working in the Bay Area from the time Ron and I married and moved from Phoenix to San Francisco. As I mentioned before, I was a freelance programmer and systems analyst after Dennis was born, and continued for six years. I worked fulltime for a local San Francisco stock brokerage firm for four years then moved to New York in 1986 to accept a job with a major financial services firm. It was the beginning of a 16 year life cycle where I went from a young, single mother of two — headstrong and outspoken, driven and determined; to an older, married grandmother of two — wiser and mellower but still outspoken, still driven and determined. It was quite a fantastic time.

The men who awed me, our leaders and executive committee members, became my peers and partners. Following in Marian's footsteps, I was the first woman in our company breaking glass ceilings and blazing a trail for others. My tomboy nature served me well. I was always confident I could do anything set before me, and for the most part that was true. It is an interesting climb up the corporate ladder. I didn't think about it much along the way. I don't remember it being a defined conscious goal until I got closer to the top. Like everyone else, I wanted to be rewarded for my achievements, reap the fruits of my labors. As in Trina Paulus' poignant book, *Hope for the Flowers*, about caterpillars climbing a pillar to nowhere, the saddest thing is to reach the top and see that there isn't any there, there, and realize that the opportunity to be a butterfly has passed by. My view of the corporate climb is described in *Corporate Ladder*.

CORPORATE LADDER

Climbing is easy
Exhilarating
Steady upward ascent.
Those below
Push me higher
Buoyed by their enthusiasm
Those above cheer me on
My successes are
Their successes.

Near the top
Rungs get narrow
Air gets thin
Oxygen competition
Brutal casualties abound
Bodies fall past me
Race to the ground.

Hands that once reached down
Helped me up
Turn to claws
Swiping at me,
Hoping I'll fall.
Feet of those who
Climbed before me
Stomp my fingers
Clinging to the upper rungs.

At the top
Vast nothingness.

A long the way up that ladder, I always felt that everyone was on my side. We had a job to do and everyone wanted to see it completed. I said in a company video we filmed for new employee orientation that the firm was somewhere where you could make a difference, somewhere that if you had an idea and a plan, you could get management support and see it to fruition. No one would hold your hand, you had to do it yourself, but they would allocate funds and get out of your way, and perhaps clap and cheer at the end. I had fun. I felt I had the respect of my peers, superiors and subordinates. It doesn't get a whole lot better when you have to work for a living.

It is said, "Be careful what you wish for." Once I was promoted and my superiors became my peers, I felt things change. I felt a fierce competition. I had built a profitable business segment that was being broken up and everyone wanted a piece of the spoils. I saw the sides of people that are never divulged down the ranks. I realized that these corporate idols were not much different than I was, which was enlightening but unsettling.

As in every company, there were shifts in responsibility and reorganizations. We went from vertical to horizontal, from divisional responsibility to co-leadership units. We went through TQM and implemented process management techniques. We hired trainers and consultants and when the market began to slide, we let them go. Throughout the changes, we all knew each other's strengths and called on them wherever and whenever needed. My knowledge and expertise often made me one of the usual suspects who served on critical committees and was involved in most major firm-wide projects. I never thought too much about being the only woman in many rooms and meetings. When I looked around, everyone looked the same to me. I suppose when others looked around, I looked somewhat out of place. Eventually a couple more women made it to the upper ranks.

Then the exclusion began. The one thing I never got used to was exclusion. It was unbearable. Without warning, I was excluded from the very groups where my knowledge was the strongest and my contribution would have been most effective. The harder I pushed back, the worse it became. I began to question my trust of others I thought were my comrades.

Once when the exclusionary tactics were so obvious and hurtful I went uptown to meet with our CEO, feeling like I had nothing to lose. I recall getting out of the subway and looking up, I saw a beautiful old church right in front of me. I was compelled to go in even though I had long since left my Catholic religion far behind me in the dust. I knelt down and immediately began crying. The thought that came to my mind was that I was experiencing discrimination for a reason. I had to feel it, really understand the insidiousness of it, to be able to change it, and help not only myself, but other women and minorities, our children and grandchildren. It was a lofty thought. The other vague thought that passed through my inner vision was that I deserved it for having had such poor judgment to engage in an in-company relationship. It was an underlying feeling of guilt and shame that was hard to shake, even though in my heart of hearts I knew the value of my contribution to the firm and I knew others knew it too.

At any rate, I pulled myself together and went to our corporate office. I was angry and so naïve. As I talked to our CEO about discrimination, he likened the situation to that of some of my male partners who had never completed college and felt less than because of it. Hello, I was *born* a woman. They chose not to finish college. I didn't feel less than, I was being treated less than. I was being discriminated against not because of my intellect or performance, but because I was not one of the boys. Whether or not that was true or was conscious behavior on the part of my colleagues, I'll never know, but that is what it felt like. I didn't think he understood. He asked me if I wanted him to fight this fight for me. I knew it was a losing battle either way, so I said no and left.

What I didn't understand until years later was that I had a part in that situation. I thought I had earned my way into the board room. I had been promoted after all. What I didn't realize was that there was some kind of initiation ritual of kissing boots or rings that I didn't quite get, but refused to learn and participate in. This bowing and junior posture that I was supposed to assume was not only foreign to me, but I see now that my ego made it impossible for me to submit to it. As a result, I was seen as not playing the game. As naïve as it sounds, I didn't really know there was a game, so I didn't know the rules. Not that I would have played if I had, but no one let me in on the deal. My experience told me that I had a job to do and to do it, without a lot of interference. Now everyone seemed to be in my business. Also, the more I felt excluded, the more I must have exuded the energy that I felt excluded, and it got worse. It was ugly and for the first time in my career I was truly not happy.

Throughout my career, I had always tried to stay true to myself, listen to my inner voice and "when in doubt, don't." During this time of exclusion and discomfort there was a situation in which I went against my better judgment and included myself without invitation. It should not have been an issue, but it was. I was humiliated and mortified, and *Party Crasher* relates it.

PARTY CRASHER

Not invited
Knowing down deep
I was not wanted,
Exclusive male
Admiration society
No room for sharing
Accomplishment
Joy
Glory.

Driven by knowing I belonged
Deserved to be included
To be a part of.
When I'm seen, they'll realize,
Their error,
Welcome me.
Faint inner voice,
"When in doubt, don't."
Ignoring my truth
I went anyway.

Surprising cool reception
Stung my cheek
Finger welts perceptible.
All eyes asked,
"What are *you* doing here?"
Wishing myself invisible
I longed to leave
I could not leave
Sin already committed.
My penance,
Stay,
Endure outcast embarrassment.

Ribbon cutting news photo
Captured my judgment error
For eternity.
Shame, humiliation
Indelibly etched
Memory neurotransmitters
Cellular level.
For years I blamed them.
Mere thought conjured
Instant emotional replay
Humiliation, anger
Surged up my back
Reddened my neck
Raced my heart.

Inner witness vision
Ego, pride clouded
Clears with
Truth-seeking willingness
Defogger.
I see my part
I accept my choices.
No victim I
No longer.

T hings improved. Time works wonders in most painful situations. Then, after a couple more reorganizations and a major
merger, our two long-term leaders were gone and the firm
changed drastically. We were laying off hundreds of people and the
morale was at an all time low. A partner was promoted. The vying
for position, protecting the chosen few, and back stabbing became
intolerable and unattractive. The atmosphere resembled an Everest
summit attempt by competing crews, without canisters. I chose dignity and retirement rather than slow death gasping for thinning air.
It was not my original plan. I didn't really have a plan, didn't think

I needed one. I had not thought about leaving, but it became the obvious alternative.

In writing to heal my knee, I forced myself to ponder the last few years of my career. I knew I had to get all the negativity out of my system in order to move on. I thought of the worst times and allowed myself to pierce the corporate veil and say what I saw, what I felt at my angriest and most hurt moments. *Soulless Raiders* is the outcome of that exercise.

SOULLESS RAIDERS

Years of free-wheeling
Money flowing autonomy
Parent company
Arrogant
Disinterested
Major sell-out coup
Just before the fall.

New global parent
First red in decades
Poor returns
Decreased market share
Jack the Knife hired
Grab profitable areas
Slash
Cut
Burn evidence.

Long private party
Over
Comfortable corporates
Ran scared
Covered asses
Protected favorites.

True colors shone through
Transparent fear.
Survival tactic
Every man
For himself.

Heads rolled
Backs were stabbed
Ruthless whispers
Ended friendships
Blood stained pedestals
Toppled.

You men
Are not my brothers
You sold your souls
You sold yourselves.
I don't know you
As I thought I did.
Don't want to know you.

As much as I was not like my partners in many ways, I was one of them. I had reaped the benefits of executive corporate management, and if they had sold their souls, so had I. As a result, I had to see my part in it, take responsibility and admit that I was not without fault, and not without blame, which I did in *Take No Prisoners*.

TAKE NO PRISONERS

Easier victim be
Point my finger
Accused, cursed perps
Take no responsibility.

Abusers
Discriminators
Excluders
Demeanors
Self-esteem strippers.
They,
They are the ones
They did it to me.

My sins
Equaled my assailants'
Yet, mirrors I consulted
Showed only their blemishes
My ruthlessness
Hidden
Behind righteousness.

Slowly, slowly
Willing
Peek around corner
Glimpse my form
In windows
As I strode by.
Glass revealed
Horrid, unsightly truths
Horns, sneers and smirks
Makeup no longer
Hides me
From me.

Once accepted
Acknowledged
My shortcomings
My dark side
Disappeared
Like shadows
On a cloudy day.
My nemesis
With a heart
Bigger than mine
Became my friend.

Hatred
Draws closer
Those we detest
Holds us captive.
Love
Breaks the spell
Ends the cycle
Sets us free.

No more than two weeks after I had decided to leave the firm, the World Trade Center crumbled. I watched the horror unfold from our office windows in Jersey City. I saw and heard too much: the second plane hit, people jumping from the tower, a new widow wailing, a survivor. I don't know how much impact that event had on my view of my life and my future, but I'm sure it had some. The images from that day stay with me. I could not write about it for quite some time. I wrote *Mind Games* on the fifth anniversary.

Mind Games

I close my eyes
As clear as day
I'm standing next to Joe
My friend and partner
We watch madness
Engulf our world
Murder in God's name.
We stand at attention
Across the Hudson
Like the landmark twins,
Straight and tall.
We watch,
One smokes and burns
Then the other sliced in two
Powerful angry bird in flight.

I'm standing with Susan,
Howling
Hysterical
Watching through a window
River and eternity
Between their outstretched hands
Her love
Her life
Returned to dust.

I'm standing
Glued to the scene
People with freedom of choice
Choose jump
Fall to their death
Rather than wait
Burn
In the high-rise pyre.

I'm standing with Helene
Her husband Bob has
Come to take her home.
He fled the scene
Crouching crawling through
Black smoke and fallen debris.
Standing in Jersey City
Lone survivor of Pompeii
Hair suit chalky grey
Face ashen
Ears full of rubble
Escapee from a Hell
Many cannot imagine.
Many more did not
Live to tell.

Paralyzed,
We who did not die
Could do nothing.
Had we been there
We could have helped
Could have saved someone.
Guilty,
For having not died
For being so helpless
We can only
Grieve.

I'm kneeling
Five years later
Thousands more dead
Thousands more to die.
A prayer for
Peace
On my lips
These images
Etched in my mind.

W hen the time came for me to leave, I had had at least four months to ponder my fate. I left with three of my partners, and the leaving soiree was a joyful affair with many friends, family and co-workers present. As I said my goodbyes, I was eternally grateful to be leaving. I felt no hatred or resentment. I realized I had an opportunity to create a whole new life. I didn't know what that would be, but I was ready to find out.

After leaving, I spent a few months just reorienting myself with my home, reestablishing my sense of place. I set no alarm clock. I had coffee in the bay window looking out at the pond. I decompressed from years of work, pressure, responsibility, and the corresponding ego and pride of status and stature. I was lost without a title, a business card, and an answer to the "What do you do?" question. For the next year, I worked on creating a career and personal development seminar with two ex-coworkers and friends, Beth and Ana. We had put quite a program together and after holding six pilot sessions we were intent on moving ahead. It was apparent that to make money at this, our main audience was major corporations. As we neared the big marketing push, I realized I couldn't do it, didn't want to do it. The parts of the seminar I enjoyed the most we were ripping out to insure its palatability to the collective corporate mind. It was painful to stop, but more painful to go on. My inability to move forward with this venture was another direct correlation to my knee pain. I couldn't run and sometimes could barely walk because I was having trouble moving forward.

A month later, I was sitting at my computer and wrote *Lonely*.

LONELY

Engulfed
In loneliness
No reason
No crisis.

I feel I have lost my way.
I have no plan for each day
I go through motions.

Elusive flitting moments
Clarity, excitement, enthusiasm
Followed by
Dull, lost loneliness.

When I had a place to go each day
I dreamed of not going
Now, I do not go, and
I do not have a dream.

I have everything
I could possibly want, need
Yet I struggle to find meaning
In the past
For the future.

I know
I can only affect today
And today
I am at sea.

Profile
Fading into a pale background
Disappearing
Returning to a voiceless
Nothingness.

Many around me
Have lost their loves
Have lost their lives
I have just
Lost my way.

In my past life
I never dreamed
I survived
Dreaming was for others.
I had responsibility
I had work to do
No time for idle thoughts.

Responsibility to be
To dream
Weighs heavy
Uncomfortable
Unfamiliar.

I know I need not
Run the streets
Looking to others for answers
As I once did.
I know the answer
My true path
Exists within
Will be revealed
When I am ready.

By the end of the summer of 2003, I enrolled in a Master's degree program at Drew University, in Medical Humanities. I earned my Master's and am over halfway through my doctorate, loving every minute of it and learning a tremendous amount. I do not have a clear picture of where this will take me, and at this time, I don't feel I have to know.

Telling My Secrets,
Healing My Pain

I f you have gotten this far, it may seem that my life has been a series of one misery after another. That is not an accurate or true picture. In fact, throughout my life I have been showered with joys beyond my wildest imaginings. Also, during even the darkest times, I could always see a ray of light, of hope, which is perhaps at the core of my good fortune.

One of the dichotomies of a good life is that feeling unsettled and unhappy when things look good seems unacceptable to society. No matter how good life is, strife and hardship befall everyone. Feelings of fear, shame, guilt, and not being good enough cut across all social barriers and may be harbored in the hearts and minds of any of us. The better our outward lives are though, the more we may feel that we have no right to sadness, mental pain, or depression. Then, these feelings of ungratefulness contribute more guilt and shame to our already overburdened shoulders, keeping us silent for far too long, and reluctant to ask for help.

I believe that the paradox of life lies in opposites. As Kahlil Gibran so beautifully wrote, in order to know joy, we must know sorrow, and tears are the prerequisite for laughter. We shed tears of pain and sorrow, yet we also shed tears when the blessings bestowed upon us overwhelm our capacity to contain joy and it wells up in our eyes and spills down our cheeks. I am so fortunate to have known that joy and to have sobbed openly in awe of the richness of life.

My greatest memories are those that not only bring a smile to my lips but make me laugh out loud. I have laughed until I cried. I have laughed until my ribs hurt and kept on laughing. I have laughed at myself, at others and with others. If I had not cried I could not have laughed as deeply. If I had never felt the pain of my heart tearing in two, I could not have felt it full and bursting with delirious delight. I could not have fallen in love again nor dropped backward to the ground to make a snow angel after dancing and spinning through our snowy backyard.

But, the joys and laughter in my life represent the opposite of the secrets and pain that must be spilled out to make room for them. I hope in time, with grace and the spell of the muse Erato about me, those joyful tears will drop from my cheeks and glisten like jewels on the pages of another book.

But first, I must finish this story, so back to my knee. Slowly, I began to be in less pain while running, but a few hours later, I would barely be able to lift up my foot. Then, the following day I would feel pretty good again, the next I would be limping. The cycle would repeat, with gradual but steady improvement over the span of probably a year. I practice yoga, and I was unable to sit back on my heels, or relax folded over in "child's pose," positions that were always second nature for me.

Now, I am virtually pain free and can do whatever I want. I no longer have any symptoms of Irritable Bowel Syndrome or colitis. I have no hip pain or lower back pain. I am aware of the tricks my mind plays, and every so often, I will get twinges here or there. I immediately review the concepts of TMS and know in my mind and heart that there is nothing physically wrong. I look hard and deep within myself and try to truthfully assess what is going on with me. Sometimes I still delude myself, but eventually the light goes on, I see and admit the truth and the symptoms and pain subside. I realize this is a lifelong cycle.

I believe that we have much more control over our bodies and our health than we think we do. The shimmering selves we are born with are ours to do with as we will. Our minds and bodies are intrinsically intertwined, contrary to Descartes' dualistic philosophy. I believe that what we think in our minds and the emotions and feelings we experience have direct impact on our bodies.

When I am suffocated by another person, I feel I cannot breathe, because I can't. When I am sad and sorrowful my heart feels like it is breaking, because it is. When I am confused and torn over decisions I have made, people I have hurt, problems I have caused, my guts feel like they're twisted, because they are. I try to recognize these signs and symptoms when they occur for what they are, a *Roadmap* for healing.

ROADMAP

I wend my way
Through my turbulent waters of denial.
Hanging, rope suspended
Hand over hand
Cross my deepest crevasses.
On my belly
Spelunk into my darkest caverns.
Blindly move forward
To my innermost thoughts
My hidden treasure
Truth of who I am
Why I am here.

At once the path is
Wide and narrow,
Dark and dank, yet
Rays of morning light slice through,
Shallow and vast with fog hanging low
Over the valley floor,
Deep with steam rising
Above pools throughout the descent,
Cold with pockets of warm fragrant air
Wafting along the way
Sweetening my journey.